The Philosophy
of Revelation

The Philosophy of Revelation

P. J. Hoedemaker

Translated and annotated by
Jan Adriaan Schlebusch

RefCon Press

The Philosophy of Revelation

Copyright © 2025

Published by **RefCon Press**
7901 4th St. North Ste. #8193
St. Petersburg, FL 33702

RefCon Press is the publishing imprint of:
The Reformed Conservative
www.thereformedconservative.org
admin@thereformedconservative.org

Originally published in Dutch by Philippus Jacobus Hoedemaker in two articles by Höveker (Amsterdam) in 1871 as "Het feit en de geschiedenis der openbaring: eene voorlezing" and "Het feit en de geschiedenis der openbaring, deel II." These articles in Dutch are in the public domain.

Library of Congress Control Number: 2025946747

ISBN: 978-1-954504-06-6 (Hardcopy)
ISBN: 978-1-954504-07-3 (eBook)

Translator: Jan Adriaan Schlebusch
General Editor: Robert J. McPherson II
Copy Editor: Paul Higgins
Cover Design: Myers Cover

To the Reformed Conservatives
Defend. Strengthen. Build.

Table of Contents

The Life and Work
of P.J. Hoedemaker

Philippus Jacobus Hoedemaker (1839–1910) was a Dutch Reformed theologian in the Anti-Revolutionary tradition; a nineteenth century philosophical tradition which, in contradistinction to the liberalism of the Enlightenment, emphasized the sovereignty of God over man and over every aspect of human life. Born in the Dutch city of Utrecht, he moved with his family to the United States at the age of thirteen in 1852, when the Hoedemakers fled what they perceived to be a Dutch government becoming increasingly hostile to traditional Christians.[1]

Indeed, in 1848 a new constitution had been accepted in the Netherlands which caused great concern for Dutch Anti-Revolutionaries, who desired to see the social order once again shaped in accordance with the principles of the Bible. The new, revised constitution did, after all, initiate a new political framework in the Netherlands where the state took control over the welfare system, seized greater control

---

[1] Daan Van Wyk, "PJ Hoedemaker: Wat ek bedoel, is die behoud van die kerk," *HTS* 46, no. 4 (1990): 501.

over children's education, and abolished Sunday-Sabbath laws.[2] The family settled in Kalamazoo, Michigan, where Hoedemaker would complete high school. Thereafter he also enrolled at Rutgers College in New Brunswick, New Jersey, in 1855, but during the second year of his studies he left the college following doubts regarding his calling. At the time, he considered a career in politics, as he had played an integral part in the successful presidential campaign of James Buchanan the year before.[3] However, such a career was not to be and he felt impelled to continue his theological studies, enrolling at a Congregationalist College in Chicago in 1858 before returning to the Europe for further study in 1861.[4]

As a student, he developed a profound interest in philosophical theology. In 1867 he graduated (*magna cum laude*) with a doctorate in divinity from Utrecht University, with the theme of his doctoral thesis being the concept of liberty in light of a theistic view of reality.[5] In his doctoral dissertation he argued that ontologically speaking, there are only two types of existence or being: independent being and dependent being. Independent being can only be attributed to God while all other realities are wholly dependent upon Him. Therefore, since there can be, logically speaking, nothing superseding or transcending the theistic, with all non-theistic or created realities being

---

[2] Jan-Willem Kirpestein, *Groen van Prinsterer als belijder van Kerk en Staat in de negentiende eeuw* (Groen & Zoon, 1993), 97.

[3] H. E. S. Woldring, *Een handvol filosofen: Geschiedenis van de filosofiebeoefening aan de Vrije Universiteit in Amsterdam van 1880 tot 2012* (Verloren, 2013), 26.

[4] George Harinck, *Mijn reis was geboden: Abraham Kuypers Amerikaanse tournee* (Verloren, 2009), 15.

[5] Ruben Alvarado, "Introduction," in Philippus Jacobus Hoedemaker, *Reformed Ecclesiology in an Age of Denominationalism*, trans. Ruben Alvarado (Pantokrator Press, 2019), ix.

necessarily dependent upon that self-existing and self-causing theistic Reality, any notions of true liberty for dependent beings as creations must necessarily be founded upon that sole self-caused and self-existing Being: the Triune God revealed in Scripture.

Hoedemaker consequently rejects any notions of liberty epistemically or ontologically developed from reason, feeling, or human will, as these are all dependent and not self-existing realities which can never logically serve as the source or foundation of true liberty.[6] Herman Bavinck beautifully articulated this same principle in his polemic against the materialism of Schopenhauer, when he argued that such non-theistic notions of reality and being entail

> that thought is not the origin of being, but being the origin of thought, which in turn entails that the central scientific presupposition that there is a logic and plan underlying reality is to be completely discarded. This presupposition can only be maintained through Christian theism which acknowledges that nature itself is the work of God and that history is the manifestation of the providential guidance of his omnipotent hand.[7]

---

[6] Philippus Jacobus Hoedmaker, *Het probleem der Vrijheid en het theïstisch godsbegrip* (Höveker, 1867), 56, 58.

[7] Herman Bavinck, *Christelijke Wetenschap* (Kok, 1904), 106. "En inderdaad, indien naar het historisch materialisme niet het denken de oorsprong is van het zijn, maar het zijn de oorsprong van het denken, dan valt in beginsel de onderstelling van alle wetenschap weg, dat er gedachte en plan, maat en getal, in de dingen schuilt. Dit is alleen te handhaven op het standpunt van het Christelijk theisme, dat ons in de natuur een werk Gods doet zien en in de geschiedenis de leiding doet erkennen van zijne almachtige hand."

During the following year, 1868, Hoedemaker would marry Johanna Horst, and together the couple would have ten children. From 1868 to 1880 he would also serve as a minister in the Dutch Reformed Church, serving the congregations of Veenendaal, Rotterdam, and Amsterdam.[8] It was during his time serving in Veenendaal that Hoedemaker befriended the well-known and increasingly influential Neo-Calvinist theologian Abraham Kuyper, eventually also accepting a teaching position as professor of philosophy at the Free University of Amsterdam, of which Kuyper was president at the time.[9] He would hold this position from 1880 to 1887. He was also named dean of the Faculty of Theology at the Free University of Amsterdam in 1882.

It is noteworthy that because of his American connections, in media reports in the United States regarding the founding of the Free University of Amsterdam, Hoedemaker actually featured more often and prominently than Kuyper himself did.[10] Nonetheless, Hoedemaker would resign from his positions at the university in 1887 due to his theological disagreements with Kuyper, after which he returned to the ministry, continuing to serve as minister in Dutch Reformed congregations until he retired in 1909, a year before his death.[11]

It is these very disagreements with Kuyper that Hoedemaker is best known for. A man of uncompromising principle, Hoedemaker viewed Kuyperian Neo-Calvinism as a deviation from its own Anti-Revolutionary principles in the sense that he considered it to be a compromise with the Enlightenment principles that it claimed to oppose. In

---

8 Van Wyk, *Hoedemaker*, 501.

9 Alvarado, "Introduction," xi.

10 Harinck, *Mijn reis*, 15.

11 Van Wyk, *Hoedemaker*, 503.

other words, he regarded the practice of Neo-Calvinism as fundamentally at odds with its own foundational premise, namely the sovereign Lordship of Jesus Christ over all areas of life. While Hoedemaker fully subscribed to the original purpose and mission of the Free University of Amsterdam, namely that Divine Revelation in the Bible ought to be the unconditional premise and foundation of human knowledge in all of the sciences, it is what he perceived to be Kuyper's deviation from these principles that lay at the heart of their disagreements.[12] On a personal level, however, Hoedemaker's split with Kuyper was something he truly lamented, as they shared a genuine mutual affection. However, when Kuyper split from the Dutch Reformed ("Hervormde") Church because of liberal theology in that denomination and consequently formed the Reformed Churches in the Netherlands, Hoedemaker opposed the move on the basis of his belief that the church should not be merely reduced to a party or club in society but serve as a spiritual home for the entire covenantal community that is the Dutch nation. A split in the church therefore entailed a split in the covenantal community, and Hoedemaker considered this problematic in light of his conviction that the purpose of the church was not to merely serve those who had come to accept true doctrine, but all members of the national covenanted community.[13] For Hoedemaker, the church is a *covenantal* and not a *contractual* institution. In other words, membership in the church came by virtue of baptism as opposed to confession. The church therefore has to remain a national institution in order to fulfill its duty toward

---

[12] Alvarado, "Introduction," xi.
[13] Van Wyk, *Hoedemaker*, 506.

the whole of the covenanted community in the sense of calling the Dutch people to national repentance.[14]

In order to fully understand Hoedemaker's ecclesiastical position in his historical context, we need to take a step back in terms of understanding the nature of the Federal Reformed tradition and in particular its opposition to liberalism in the eighteenth and nineteenth centuries. In the Federal or Covenantal tradition, which had most excellently been embodied by the Swiss Reformer Heinrich Bullinger (1504–75), the Christian nation was, in essence, to be considered a covenantal community in relation to Christ as covenantal head. In light of this, true national prosperity is also seen by Bullinger as dependent upon obedience to God's commandments in his Word.[15] This conception regarding the covenantal origin and nature of nationhood in relation to God as Creator played a decisive role in the historical-political development of Western nations such as Switzerland, Great Britain, America, Hungary, and South Africa prior to the rise of social contract theory with the eighteenth-century Enlightenment.[16] This social contract theory fundamentally did away with this conception of society, in turn advocating a strictly individualistic social ontology in which society is seen as constituted by virtue of the free association of naturally sovereign individuals who, in sacrificing

---

[14] Philippus Jacobus Hoedemaker, *Heel de kerk en heel de volk! Een protest tegen het optreden der Gereformeerden als partij, en een Woord van afscheid aan de Confessionele Vereeniging* (Sneek, 1897), 6, 10.

[15] Heinrich Bullinger, *Anklag und erstliches ermanen Gottes Allmachtigen zu eyner gemeynnen Eydgenosschaft*, (Froschauer, 1544), 7, 52.

[16] Charles McCoy and Wayne Baker, *Fountainhead of Federalism: Heinrich Bullinger and the Covenantal Tradition* (Westminster/John Knox, 1991), 27.

their sovereignty, delegate it to the state for the sake of making human society possible.[17] The nature of this theory's deviation from Biblical principles was superbly articulated by the Southern Presbyterian philosopher-theologian Robert Lewis Dabney, who wrote:

> The claim of a social contract is [a] theory [that] is atheistic and unchristian. Such were Hobbes and the Jacobins. It is true that Locke tried to hold it in a Christian sense, but it is none the less obstinately atheistic in that it wholly discards God, man's relation to Him, His right to determine our condition and moral existence, and the great fact of moral philosophy, that God has formed and ordained us to live under civil government ... [In terms of the social contract] civil society is herself a grand robber of my natural rights, which I only tolerate to save myself from other more numerous robbers. How then can any of the rules of government be an expression of essential morality? ... Commonwealths have not historically begun in such an optional compact of lordly savages. Such absolute savages, could we find any considerable number of them, would not usually possess the good sense and the self-control which would be sufficient for any permanent good. The only real historical instances of such compacts have been the agreements of outlaws forming companies of banditti, or crews of pirate ships. Those combinations realize precisely the ideals pictured by Hobbes, Locke, and Rousseau. Did ever one of them result in the

---

[17] John Locke, *The Second Treatise of Civil Government*, ed. Andrew Baily (Broadview Press, 2015), 93.

creation of a permanent and well-ordered commonwealth? The well-known answer to this question hopelessly refutes the scheme. Commonwealths have usually arisen, in fact, from the expansion of clans, which were at first but larger families.[18]

Indeed, it can be said that Hoedemaker dedicated his life's work to the same cause as his contemporary, Dabney, albeit on the opposite side of the Atlantic. As the Dutch Dabney, Hoedemaker's ecclesiastical struggle was characterized by the same resistance and opposition to the Jacobin egalitarianism's destructive impact upon society.

Hoedemaker's view of the church and of civil government was furthermore much more in line with that of his predecessor, Groen van Prinsterer, than Kuyper's. Like Groen, Hoedemaker exhibited a similar sympathy with those who had left the national Dutch Reformed Church because of theological liberalism, but had serious reservations regarding the implications of such a split. The *Afgescheidenen* ("Separated"), as the first Dutch split-off denomination of the 1830s became known, had asked the Dutch government at the time for civil authorization, which Groen denounced as a concession to state absolutism.[19] For both Groen and Hoedemaker, the state and the church are fundamentally covenantal institutions designed and willed by God for the protection, sanctification, and preservation of the Dutch nation as covenantal community under the authority of and in relationship with God. Without the national church, therefore, the

---

[18] Robert L. Dabney, *Discussions, Volume III: Philosophical* (Presbyterian Committee of Publication, 1892), 308–9.

[19] Guillaume Groen van Prinsterer, *Nederlandsche Gedachten, 2nd series—V* (Höveker, 1873), 292–93.

nation's continued existence would be under threat and any tendencies to elevate the authority of the state over that of the church had to be vigorously opposed as the fruits of Enlightenment liberalism.

This same principle would later also place Hoedemaker in direct opposition to Kuyper on another major issue relating to Article 36 of the Belgic Confession of Faith, one of the main doctrinal standards in the Dutch Reformed tradition, which addresses the doctrine of civil government. Kuyper came to believe in the pluralistic principle of freedom of religion, which Hoedemaker countered was not only something very different, but very much at odds with the traditional principle of freedom of conscience.[20] Kuyper's position led him to advocate for the removal of a phrase from the article which states that Christian civil magistrates should "remove and prevent all idolatry and false worship, that the kingdom of the antichrist may be thus destroyed."

Kuyper countered that this was beyond the God-given duties of the state, and that the state had to tolerate the practice of false religions in the context of a pluralistic society.[21] In 1896 Kuyper and Bavinck, along with a number of other leading theologians at the time, recommended to the general synod of the Reformed Churches in the Netherlands that this phrase be removed from the Belgic Confession, a request to which the synod of 1905 eventually complied.[22] Hoedemaker, to the contrary, maintained

---

[20] Ruben Alvarado, "Preface," in Philippus Jacobus Hoedemaker, *Article 36 of the Belgic Confession Vindicated against Dr. Abraham Kuyper: A Critique of his Series on Church and State in "Common Grace"*, trans. Ruben Alvarado (Pantokrator Press, 2019), xvi.
[21] Ibid., xiii.
[22] Cornelius Van Dam, *God and Government. Biblical Principles for Today—An Introduction and Resource* (Wipf & Stock, 2011), 54.

a distinctly theonomic view of the role and duty of civil government.

For Hoedemaker, any deviation from the original wording of Article 36 of the Belgic Confession would "prove destructive for the Church, the state, the country and the nation." as it violates the principle that government ought to rule in accordance with the "truth of ... God's commandments."[23] For this reason, Hoedemaker maintained, the civil government ought to use its authority to punish openly blasphemous or public violations of the first table of God's Law.[24] In this regard Hoedemaker, more so than Kuyper, has to be considered the true heir of the Anti-Revolutionary political theory of their predecessor Groen van Prinsterer, as the latter also held that the state, as divinely-instituted structure of authority, ought to use "legal means to punish blasphemy."[25]

In other words, unlike Kuyper (and Bavinck), Hoedemaker simply refused to make any compromise with the egalitarianism found at the heart of the dispute regarding religious freedom in the public domain. While valuing liberty of conscience, he maintained that Christ could not be regarded as merely one of many gods legally worshiped in public life, since this would amount to a violation of His Lordship over all of creation.[26] Here again, we find Hoedemaker engaging in the same battle and at the same time in the Netherlands as Dabney did in America.

---

[23] Philippus Jacobus Hoedemaker, *Nationaal niet clericaal* (Sneek, 1897), 20, 26. "Kerk, Staat, Land en Volk verwoest," "de waarheid van ... de Goddelijke ordonnantiën."

[24] Hoedemaker, *Nationaal niet clericaal*, 17.

[25] Guillaume Groen van Prinsterer, *Handboek der Geschiedenis van het Vaderland, vol. I* (Höveker, 1852), 73: "door wettige middelen, door bestraffen van hetgeen godslasterlijk is."

[26] Hoedemaker, *Nationaal*, 34.

Dabney, in writing against the secularization (or rather de-Christianization) of education, "there is but one ground of moral obligation, the will of God" upon which legitimate government is dependent and "therefore it enforces the Sabbath [and] punishes blasphemy," which itself invalidates all notions of religious equality in the public domain, since there can be no neutrality between Christianity and opposing religions.[27] Divine Revelation was, in contradistinction to Kuyper, held by Hoedemaker to be the sole source of authority and ultimate moral standard, not only for the family and the church, but also for the state. Hoedemaker therefore, like Dabney, exhibited a distinct love for his country and his people just as much as the Church, and dedicated his life toward advocating for the Lordship of Christ—in practice and not only in theory—over every area of Dutch cultural and national life.[28]

At the very heart of this famous dispute and break between Hoedemaker and Kuyper regarding the practical implications of Christ's Lordship for the public domain, however, was Hoedemaker's philosophy of Revelation. For Hoedemaker, Kuyper's idea that a common grace ought to light the path of civil government, as opposed to special grace which guides the church, amounted to a fundamentally epistemological problem: it falsely dichotomized revealed and natural knowledge, which Hoedemaker countered with the idea that all human knowledge, whether it pertains to the ecclesiastical or the civil realm, is dependent upon God not only for its

---

[27] Robert Lewis Dabney, *On Secular Education* (Canon Press, 1996), 10, 19.

[28] Daan Van Wyk, "P J Hoedemaker, teoloog en kerkman," *HTS* 47, no. 4 (1991): 1069.

epistemic Revelation to man, but for its very ontological existence as created facts or realities.[29]

And that brings us to the main focus of this book: Hoedemaker's philosophy of Revelation.

The Hoedemakerian Philosophy of Revelation

When we think of the philosophy of Revelation in the context of the Reformed tradition, perhaps the most well-known work that immediately comes to mind is the series of Stone Lectures held by Herman Bavinck under this very title at Princeton University in 1908. Despite sharing Hoedemaker's understanding of Divine Revelation as essentially amounting to a sovereign God speaking and acting in the history of his creation, as well as that Revelation being foundational to not only all knowledge but also to the existence of creation itself,[30] Bavinck does not mention Hoedemaker even once during the lectures. This, despite the latter having a highly developed philosophy of Revelation which Bavinck most certainly was familiar with. After all, in 1886, while Hoedemaker was still professor at the Free University of Amsterdam and Bavinck professor of Dogmatics at the Theological University of Kampen, Bavinck had also expressed his appreciation for Hoedemaker's view of Scripture.[31] The reasons for Bavinck's lack of recognition of Hoedemaker will be treated below, but first, it is vital to provide a summary of the most central tenets of the Hoedemakerian philosophy of Revelation.

---

[29] Alvarado, "Preface," xv.

[30] Philippus Jacobus Hoedemaker, *Christus voor de rechtbank: der moderne wetenschap* (Daamen, 1898), 28; Herman Bavinck, *Wijsbegeerte der Openbaring* (Kok, 1908), 23.

[31] Herman Bavinck, "Review van 'Niet van eigen uitlegging' door P.J. Hoedemaker," *De Bazuin* 34, no. 51 (1886).

First, for Hoedemaker Divine Revelation is holistic, universal, and inescapable. It encompasses not only all knowledge and facts, but all of created reality of which God is the absolute first cause. As such Hoedemaker makes no hard distinction between special Revelation and general Revelation or abstract Revelation and historical Revelation. In fact, for Hoedemaker, there is not a single fact in the universe whatsoever that is not dependent upon and mediated by Divine Revelation. All that is true about anything falls within the scope of Revelation, not only on an epistemological level, but also on an ontological level, that is, reality is not only something we come to know and understand by Revelation, but it is, for its very existence, dependent upon God as the Divine Energy or ultimate First Cause behind everything in existence.[32]

Since God is the only fully independent, self-existing, and all-causing Reality, all dependent realities in distinction to Him are necessarily based on the Revelation of His will.[33] This holistic view of Revelation does not imply that Hoedemaker does not acknowledge the unique character of special Revelation, however. He recognizes its infallibility, but even this infallibility finds its meaning within the context of its historical context. In other words, God's written Word is not a set of abstract truths, but the propositions of the text itself are historically mediated.[34] In this regard Bavinck also deviates from Hoedemaker. For Bavinck,

---

[32] Philippus Jacobus Hoedemaker, *Eenvoudige onderwijzing in de christelijke leer naar de belijdenis der Hervormde Kerk* (Sneek, 1892), 20; Philippus Jacobus Hoedemaker, *Het feit en de geschiedenis der openbaring: eene voorlezing* (Höveker, 1871), 15.

[33] Hoedemaker, *theïstisch godsbegrip*, 147.

[34] Hoedemaker, *Eenvoudige onderwijzing*, 32–33.

> The specific distinction between Israel's religion and the religions of the pagans cannot be traced back to the concept of revelation. It cannot be reduced to a distinction between *religio revelata* (revealed religion) and *religio naturalis* (natural religion). The *religio naturalis* is no religion but a philosophy. Religions are positive, i.e. they rely upon a real or apparent revelation. Rather, the truly material difference can be found in the gratia.[35]

In this regard Bavinck distanced himself not only from Hoedemaker but also from his Anti-Revolutionary predecessor Groen van Prinsterer, who argued:

> How much wisdom, they say, did the ancients not possess! Certainly, but this was not knowledge in the sense that is often attributed to natural religion. Their foundational convictions were derived from traditional beliefs and their highest wisdom consisted in distinguishing those truths of the original divine revelation from the superstitions of the common people as well as the clergy.[36]

---

[35] Herman Bavinck, *De algemeene genade* (Zalsman, 1894), 11. "Het specifieke onderscheid tusschen Israels godsdienst en de godsdiensten der volken kan daarom niet gelegen zijn in het begrip der openbaring. Het kan niet weergegeven worden door de tegenstelling van religio revelata (geopenbaarde godsdienst) en religio naturalis (natuurlijke godsdienst). De religio naturalis is geen godsdienst maar wijsbegeerte. Alle religies zijn positief: zij berusten op werkelijke of vermeende openbaring. Maar het eigentlijke, materieele verschil ligt in de gratia."

[36] Guillaume Groen van Prinsterer, *Beschouwingen over staats- en volkenrecht, I: Proeve over de middelen waardoor de waarheid wordt gekend en gestaafd* (S & J Luchtmans, 1834), 36–37.

For Groen, the fact that all people descend from the first ancestors means that, through their ancestors and hence through their traditions, they have access to the original proto-gospel of special Revelation.

Second, for Hoedemaker, Revelation, as historically mediated, has a distinctly narrative character. Hoedemaker's claim that "Revelation is historical"[37] needs to be understood within the context of his nineteenth-century struggle against epistemological rationalism. Hoedemaker was a true counter-Enlightenment Anti-Revolutionary, and as such, ever eager to emphasize the pedagogic value of history over against rationalistic conceptions of natural law as abstraction.[38]

However, his emphasis on the historical nature of all Revelation amounts to much more than a mere polemic against rationalist or empiricist abstractions. For Hoedemaker, Revelation is narrational or "historical" because reality as such is narrational or historical. In order to understand what I mean by this, allow me to utilize, as a means of understanding Hoedemaker, the philosophy of history of one of the great twenty-first century historiographers, American David Carr (1940–). When the reader comes across the idea of a "narrative" approach to anything, you may be tempted to think about the postmodern

---

"Hoeveel, zegt men, was ook aan de wijsgeeren der oudheid bekend! Voorzeker; maar dit niet in dien zin, welke men er doorgaans aan geeft, natuurlijke Godsdienst geweest. Hunne gronddenkbeelden waren uit het traditionele geloof overgenomen, en hun hoogste wijsheid heeft hierin bestaan, dar zij het goud der oorspronkelijk geopenbaarde waarheid somtijds van het schuim der volksbijgeloovigheden en priestervonden wisten te ontdoen."

[37] Hoedemaker, *Het feit en de geschiedenis*, 14–15.

[38] W. G. F. Van Vliet, *Groen van Prinsterers Historische benadering van de politiek* (Verloren, 2008), 29–32.

notion of reducing all truth or fact to a subjective or manmade concepts. However, Carr's narrative realism is very much distinct and in opposition to the narrative anti-realism of postmodernism. While postmodern narratives essentially reduce these to fiction, Carr has argued that narrative is inherent to human participation in and experience of reality as such. In other words, narrative itself forms the framework which provides sense and meaning to human existence, in which the present can only be understood in light of the past and of an envisaged future.[39] There is an inherent historicity to human existence, which can only be understood within the narrative framework provided by the perpetual interplay of past, present and future.[40]

This is exactly how the historical nature of Revelation needs to be understood with Hoedemaker. To him, it is through Revelation, as a historical reality, that we understand and interpret the facts of Revelation in the present, and these facts are not merely abstractions, but life-changing facts, revealed to us by the Holy Spirit with the purpose of engaging in the world for the glory of God and with an eschatological vision for the future. Facts, therefore, find their meaning and coherence within the inescapable narrative framework provided by God's sovereign providence over and plan for Creation as this manifests in world history.

Therefore, facts are never brute theory, as if this could be ever separated from practical reality, but revealed facts always manifest through the Revelation of the historical and providentially ordained realities in relation to their origin in God as Creator and their

---

[39] David Carr, *Experience and History: Phenomenological Perspectives on the Historical World* (Oxford University Press, 2014), 67–68.

[40] Carr, *Experience and History*, 134.

fulfillment in the divine purpose of creation, the Lordship of Christ.[41] In other words, revealed facts are non-abstract historical realities because all of creation as such is a non-abstract historical reality.[42] Because of this, all facts are inescapably God-given facts to be discovered by means of the reception of Divine Revelation and to be understood within the framework of that Revelation. Facts can never be invented by means of human ingenuity, never be imprinted on a blank slate by the senses, and never be rightly understood as abstractions.

Thirdly, while the facts of Revelation are, in an objective sense, narrative or historical, the Object of Revelation, God Himself, is not. God, as self-existing and eternal Being, cannot be reduced to a historical fact. Thus, while all facts and truths are mediated to us through Revelation as a historical phenomenon, God Himself cannot be reduced to a historical phenomenon, because of His eternal and self-existent nature and because He is the ultimate and uncaused First Cause of all that exists independently of Himself. In other words, Revelation and all of its truths come to man as historically given realities, but God Himself, as the sovereign Giver thereof, is a supra-historical, eternal Being, the Source of all such realities.[43] In other words, facts, derived from the Latin word *facere*, which means "to create," stand in an undeniable and inescapable relation to their eternal Source, their Creator-God. Thus, Hoedemaker's philosophy of Revelation is fundamentally shaped by a clear and hard ontological distinction between Creator and creation as not only two mutually exclusive realities, but also two ontologically exhaustive realities, that is, the two realities which encompasses all existence.

---

[41] Hoedemaker, *Het feit en de geschiedenis*, 22–23.

[42] Ibid., 19.

[43] Ibid., 30.

Fourthly, Revelation is a redemptive reality—one that holistically redeems all created realities. Revelation's historical progress is not only a theoretical progress, but a very practical and redemptive progress. It is not only the knowledge of God itself that is progressively mediated by virtue of His sovereign direction of history, but in particular its redemptive impact upon humanity and creation which manifests in accordance with the teleological purposes of divine design. God redeems the world through Christ, the supreme Object of Revelation, but Revelation itself serves as a providential means by which God carries out the work of redemption and applies it to the subjects of that Revelation. Its redemptive significance is also covenantal, since it is by virtue of the covenantal relationship with God that man, by virtue of God's historical works of creation and redemption, subjectively appropriates the truth of Revelation through the power of the Holy Spirit. In other words, as true knowledge of God and of his creation is progressively revealed, this knowledge changes the hearts and minds of humans—as primary second causes in world history—and consequently, through the changing of hearts and minds, humanity is covenantally redeemed and, by the power of the Holy Spirit, brought to accord with the divine will to expand Christ's Kingdom, and so consequently become themselves teleologically orientated toward that very purpose.

Finally, because Revelation is historical and redemptive, it is also inherently eschatological. Of all the great Dutch Reformed theologians of the eighteenth and early-nineteenth centuries (including Groen van Prinsterer, Kuyper, and Bavinck) Hoedemaker understood this the best. Revealed facts are not only inseparable from their origin in God, but also from their fulfillment in Christ. For Hoedemaker, the future, like the past, needs to be understood in terms of God's redemptive purpose for all of creation in and through Christ. The purpose of history as mediator of Divine Revelation is to sanctify all of creation under the Lordship of Christ.[44] In other words, because the facts of Revelation are not abstract but historical realities, they always serve God's purpose and plan with all of history. Every thought must be taken captive in obedience to Christ. For Hoedemaker, "true science is Christocentric" precisely because all facts find their origin, meaning, and fulfillment in Him (2 Corinthians 10:5).[45] In this regard, Hoedemaker's eschatology had a distinctly postmillennial character in that he foresaw a time in future when all the nations of the world would be brought in obedience to Christ through the redemptive power of the facts of Revelation.

As mentioned earlier, Herman Bavinck systematically laid out his philosophy of Revelation in a series of Stone Lectures held at Princeton University in 1908, two years prior to Hoedemaker's death, without mentioning him even once. Bavinck had sided with Kuyper against Hoedemaker with regard to the issue of whether civil government has the right and duty to outlaw idolatry and blasphemy in the public domain. Underlying their dispute, however, was a distinct difference in the philosophy of Revelation itself, to which we will now turn.

While Bavinck agreed with Hoedemaker that Revelation is organic and historical in nature, he did not understand this to imply that it has a distinctly non-abstract character. For Bavinck, any wholesale rejection of rationalism when it comes to the reception and understanding of Revelation disregards the importance of "personal independence."[46] In this,

---

[44] Hoedemaker, *Het feit en de geschiedenis*, 37.

[45] Hoedemaker, *Christus voor de regtbank*, xii: "De ware wetenschap is christocentrish."

[46] Bavinck, *Wijsbegeerte*, 145–46: "persoonlijke zelfstandigheid."

Bavinck's rejection of the rationalism underlying Schleiermacher's higher criticism was more eclectic than that of Hoedemaker. This is because, for Bavinck, there exists an unmediated knowledge of self-being or self-existence in self-consciousness. For him, those universally shared axiomata underlying the belief in the reliability of observations made by the senses amounts to an "immediate form of knowledge" locked up in our "self-consciousness."[47] Bavinck therefore claims that when it comes to self-consciousness, "Kant was right inasmuch as he articulated the autonomy of human knowing and acting."[48]

This does not imply that Bavinck should be considered a Kantian, however. He certainly borrowed concepts from Kant, but also successfully argued against the Kantian epistemological boundary between consciousness and reality by arguing that the external world and our consciousness thereof only correspond because both are united as creations of a single sovereign God and as such products of a single divine will.[49] He also rejected the Kantian dichotomy between faith and knowledge and argued that the Christian worldview alone is able to reconcile the two.[50] Nonetheless, following Kant, Bavinck did allow for a distinction between the epistemic qualities of faith on the one hand and knowledge on the other, as well as for a distinction between their respective objects, Revelation, and facts. He writes, for example, that

> that which I know, I believe, but not all that I believe, I know. Oftentimes we can only argue

---

47 Bavinck, *Christelijke Wetenschap*, 37, 53: "onmiddelijk weten," "zelfbewustzijn."

48 Bavinck, *Wijsbegeerte*, 64: "inzoover was Kant in zijn recht, als hij de autonomie van het kennen en handelen des menschen uitsprak."

49 Bavinck, *Christelijke Wetenschap*, 72.

50 Ibid., 31, 43, 58.

> that it is not foolish to believe in divine revelation, but foolish indeed to not believe it. Here on earth we never ascend beyond faith, which will only be rewarded with knowledge through sight in heaven ... That which we [now] truly know is very little, as Kant and Comte have convincingly shown.[51]

For Bavinck, while not in terms of subjective certainty, but still "in terms of objective evidence, faith stands below knowledge."[52] He even goes as far as to claim that "which religious faith is to be considered right and truthful ... must be made out by each individual personally in his conscience before God."[53] In this regard Bavinck, albeit in a more nuanced fashion, maintained a similar distinction to that of Kuyper between natural and evident knowledge on the one hand, and that which is revealed and accepted by faith on the other. Kuyper even goes as far as to argue that

> the *revelatio specialis* is unthinkable without presupposing the *theologia naturalis*, since grace does not create a single new reality...In

---

[51] Bavinck, *Christelijke Wetenschap*, 16–17, 43: "Wat ik weet, geloof ik; maar niet alles wat ik geloof, weet ik. Dikwerf kunnen wij het alleen zoover brengen, dat wij aantoonen, dat het niet dwaas is, de openbaring te gelooven, maar wel dwaas, om het tegenoverstelde aan te nemen. Nimmer komen wij hier op aarde dus het standpunt des geloofs te boven. Eerst in den hemel ontvangt het geloof in de kennis door aanschouwing zijn loon ... Wat wij werkelijk kennen, is gering in inhoud en klein in omvang. Kant en Comte hebben ons daarvan diep doordrongen."

[52] Ibid., 45: "in objectieve evidentie staat het gelooven beneden het weten."

[53] Ibid., 94: "welke godsdienstig geloof het ware en zuivere is ... moet ten slotte door ieder persoonlijk, in zijn geweten, voor God worden uitgemaakt."

regeneration there is no new substance added to the essence of man, which has not been endowed to him by virtue of creation.[54]

For Kuyper, like Bavinck, natural knowledge forms the necessary interpretative framework for faith in Divine Revelation, since the first rests on a more immediate self-consciousness.

Of such concession to the epistemology of empiricism or rationalism, Hoedemaker would have nothing. For him, this amounted to ascribing to the human mind an independence that man, as dependent being, could never achieve. Hoedemaker rejects any kind of distinction between faith and knowledge, since all knowledge is necessarily mediated through Divine Revelation. In refuting Kant, Hoedemaker argues that the existence of any self-consciousness already presupposes a consciousness of that which is not the self, which negates the possibility of any unrevealed or autonomous knowledge.[55] In other words, since man is a created being, any self-consciousness on the part of man can only come into existence within a created framework provided and revealed by God as Creator, ultimate First Cause and Sovereign Ruler of all things.

But this diversion between Hoedemaker on the one hand and Kuyper and Bavinck on the other, also had profound implications for their respective political theories and especially with regard to their aforementioned dispute regarding Article 36 of the

---

54 Abraham Kuyper, *Encyclopaedie der heilige godgeleerdheid, tweede deel: Algemeen deel* (Kok, 1909), 327: "de revelatio specialis geen ogenblijk denkbaar is zonder de onderstelling der theologia naturalis, ligt eenvoudig hieraan, dat de gratia nooit één enkele nieuwe realiteit schept ... In de wedergeboorte wordt aan's menschen wezen niet een nieuw bestanddeel, dat in de schepping buiten ons wezen lag, aan ons wezen toegevoegd."
55 Hoedemaker, *theïstisch godsbegrip*, 136.

Belgic Confession. The idea of an unmediated knowledge on the part of man enabled Kuyper to distinguish between what he understood to be natural knowledge and that which he considered to be revealed knowledge, arguing that the former and not the latter should be the guide and standard for legislation and public policy.[56] To the contrary, Hoedemaker, not adhering to any dichotomy between natural and revealed knowledge, maintained that God's Law should remain the moral standard for all civil governments, since true knowledge of God acquired through nature can never be at odds with the principles set out in Scripture.[57] Redeeming all of creation for God's glory, after all, necessitates that it be done in accordance with the revealed will of the sovereign God of that creation.

The Anti-Revolutionaries and Presuppositionalists

The similarities between the epistemology of nineteenth-century Anti-Revolutionaries such as Hoedemaker and Groen van Prinsterer with the twentieth-century Presuppositionalism of thinkers such as Cornelius Van Til (1895—1987), Gordon Clark (1902—85), and Herman Dooyeweerd (1894—1977) is undeniably striking. Like the later Presuppositionalists, the Anti-Revolutionaries also emphasized the inescapability of pre-theoretical commitments of faith or presuppositions when it comes to interpreting reality. Groen van Prinsterer, for example, famously noted:

---

[56] Abraham Kuyper, *Ons Program* (J. A. Wormser, 1892), 79.

[57] Philippus Jacobus Hoedemaker, *Handboek voor het onderwijs in het Oude Testament ten dienste van het catechisatie, het huisgezin en de zondagschool* (Höveker, 1886), 30–31.

All scientific investigation is necessarily and inescapably founded upon first principles. Regardless of the subject under investigation, at the start of the research there are certain accepted truths upon which the study itself is dependent. These truths ensure the stability of the scientific building and without these truths the results of such investigations can only be delusions. So it is with all science, so it is with law. All research and presentation are in vain, when it is not founded upon solid ground ... What are principles? Principles are accepted truths by which every investigation is enabled, i.e. acknowledged truths that form the foundation of every argument. These truths can often in themselves be conclusions derived from higher truths. In this way we can climb up from high principles to even higher principles, until we acquire the highest truths, which are indubitable, yet not subject to scrutiny—objects of faith, which is the starting point of any science. These are the principles which are rooted in God's will and nature par excellence.[58]

---

[58] Guillaume Groen van Prinsterer, *Beschouwingen over staats-en volkenrecht, I: Proeve over de middelen waardoor de waarheid wordt gekend en gestaafd* (S & J Luchtmans, 1834), 1, 3: "Elke wetenschap heeft eigen beginsels. Hoedanig de kring der onderwerpen ze behandelt, aan het hoofd des onderzoeks staan waarheden die ten rigtsnoer verstrekken en waarvan zij de ontwikkeling en toepassing bevat. Deze maken de vastheid uit van het wetenschappelijk gebouw; zonder haar worden luchtkasteelen gesticht. Zoo is het met elke wetenschap; zoo met staats- en volkenrecht. Onderzoek en betoog zijn ijdel, indien ze niet rusten op onwrikbaren grond ... Wat zijn beginsels? Beginsels zijn waarheden, met welke het onderzoek begint; erkende waarheden, die ten

This exact same sentiment was of course later echoed by Presuppositionalists such as Gordon Clark, who writes:

> Every philosophic or theological system must begin somewhere, for if it did not begin it would not continue. But a beginning cannot be preceded by anything else, or it would not be a beginning. Therefore, every system must be based on presuppositions (required as a precondition of possibility and coherence, tacitly assumed to be the case) or axioms (an accepted statement or proposition regarded as being self-evidently true). They may be Spinoza's axioms; they may be Locke's sensory starting point, or whatever. Every system must therefore be presuppositional. The first principle cannot be demonstrated because there is nothing prior from which to deduce it.[59]

Likewise, Hoedemaker's rejection of the autonomous mind was later echoed by both Van Til and Dooyeweerd, who both vehemently denied the idea of autonomous reason. For Dooyeweerd all human knowledge is dependent upon the acceptance of pre-theoretical intuitions and non-demonstrable commitments of faith as the necessary framework

---

grondslage der redenering worden gelegd. Deze waarheden kunnen zelve gevolgtrekkingen en uit hooger waarheden afgeleid zijn. Zoo klimt men van hooger tot hooger beginselen op, tot men de hoogste waarheden bereikt, ontwijfelbaar, doch onvatbaar voor ontleding en betoog; voorwerpen van een geloof, dat het begin der wetenschap is. Deze heeten bij uitnemendheid beginsels en zijn in Gods wil en wezen gegrond."

[59] Gordon Clark, *A Christian Philosophy of Education* (Eerdmans, 1946), 41.

enabling theoretical thinking because the presuppositional nature of human thought or experience pertains to the innate human impulse to direct itself toward the absolute origin, source, and cause of all meaning, and as such presuppositions are pre-theoretical and non-demonstrable commitments taken on faith.[60] Van Til likewise argued that God and His Revelation, as opposed to man himself, ought to be "the ultimate reference point in human predication."[61]

Nonetheless, despite these significant agreements there is also a notable difference between the Christian-Historical epistemology of the eighteenth-century Dutch Anti-Revolutionaries and the twentieth-century American Presuppositionalism embodied by Van Til and Clark as well as the Amsterdam School of Dooyeweerd. While both the Anti-Revolutionaries and the Presuppositionalists reject the natural law doctrine of the Thomists, the former school exhibits a far greater appreciation for classical thought than the latter. This can be attributed to the differences between what is commonly called the "historicist" element in Anti-Revolutionary theory and the "rationalist" element in Presuppositionalism. Both schools vehemently reject empiricism—the idea that observations of natural phenomena can ever be considered normative. However, Van Til famously posits that "no form of natural theology has ever spoken properly of the God that is there."[62] In light thereof Van Til concluded that none of the ancient

---

[60] Herman Dooyeweerd, *De wijsbegeerte der wetsidee. Boek I: De wetsidee als grondlegging der wijsbegeerte* (H. J. Paris, 1935), 21, 24.

[61] Cornelius Van Til, *The Defense of the Faith* (Presbyterian and Reformed Publishing, 1967), 180.

[62] Cornelius Van Til's letter to Francis Schaeffer, March 11, 1969, in *Ordained Servant* 6, no. 4 (1997): 77.

pagan philosophers could not have spoken truths concerning God or His Revelation of creation because they start with autonomous reason. Like Van Til, Groen van Prinsterer, in following the Canons of Dort III/IV.4, also rejects natural theology as being at enmity with God because of human depravity,[63] but despite this, takes a far more positive stance on the wisdom of the ancients. He writes:

> The truths ascribed to natural religion are supposedly confirmed by reason and this natural religion is said to be rational. How much wisdom, they claim, was not known by the ancient philosophers! Undoubtedly, but these basic truths were derived from the traditional religion of their ancestors. Their highest wisdom consisted in their ability to, at times, distinguish these truths of the religion originally revealed from the froth of their national superstitions and the doctrines originating from their priests. Religion is traditional. Knowledge of the true God could not arise with the rough natural man, as the false philosophies propose.[64]

---

[63] Groen van Prinsterer, *Proeve*, 36.

[64] Ibid., 36-7: "Hoeveel, zegt men, was ook aan de wijsgeeren der oudheid bekend! Voorzeker; maar dit niet in dien zin, welke men er doorgaans aan geeft, natuurlijke Godsdienst geweest. Hunne gronddenkbeelden waren uit het traditionele geloof overgenomen, en hun hoogste wijsheid heeft hierin bestaan, dar zij het goud der oorspronkelijk geopenbaarde waarheid somtijds van het schuim der volksbijgeloovigheden en priestervonden wisten te ontdoen. Alle Godsdienst is traditioneel. Het denkbeeld van God zou bij het ruwen natuurmensch, gelijk de valsche wijsbegeerte dien voorstelt, nooit opgekomen zijn."

Hoedemaker follows this exact same line of reasoning when he denies the distinction between revealed and natural knowledge altogether.[65] For Hoedemaker, all knowledge is intrinsically bound to God's Revelation of Himself and His will, and because He is absolutely sovereign, there is not a single unrevealed fact in the universe.[66]

Their appreciation for ancient wisdom needs to be understood in terms of their view of knowledge as historicist or traditional. For them Revelation is mediated through history. As Christian historicists they hold that all people, including the ancient Greeks and Romans, have ancestors to whom the true proto-Gospel was revealed (since all people descend from Adam and Noah), and that their knowledge and wisdom are due to the remnants thereof that were passed down through generations by means of tradition. For this reason, there are also common moral and theological truths that are recognized as such by all religions. Within this framework, the emergence of all non-Christian religions and philosophies to phenomena that can be traced back to the sinful nature of humans, who tend to distort the original revealed truths of God.

Dooyeweerd famously critiqued this historicist approach by arguing that Christian historicism risked oversimplifying the complex interplay of human actions and divine sovereignty. He believed that historical events could not be directly equated with divine acts or intentions but should be understood within a framework of multiple modal aspects that reflect the diverse ways in which God's order is

---

65 Hoedemaker, *Handboek*, 30.

66 Hoedemaker, *onderwijzing*, 15.

expressed in the world.[67] Dooyeweerd maintains that Groen and Hoedemaker's Christian historicism cultivates a relativist vision where there is no place for constant and unchangeable norms and standards or clear boundaries between spheres. The emphasis on culturally and historically developed rights is something which Dooyeweerd regards as at odds with the eternal structural-principles of society, rooted in creation and according to which all the states of all the peoples should be ordered, per Dooyeweerd. He vehemently rejects this particularist emphasis of Christian historicism, even maintaining that "it was the historical school which propagated the false idea that civil law is essentially rooted in national identity, which paved the way for the rise of National Socialism with its racialist ideology."[68]

At the heart of this difference between the twentieth-century Presuppositionalists and the nineteenth-century Anti-Revolutionaries lies their differing views regarding the epistemic role of tradition. Both reject rationalism and both reject empiricism, but the nineteenth-century Anti-Revolutionaries embody more of a Romanticist polemic stance against the Enlightenment's rejection of tradition—something that is generally missing from the works of the later Presuppositionalists. In this regard the Anti-Revolutionaries represent a view that could be described as Presuppositionalist Traditionalism in contradistinction to the Scripturalism embodied by the

---

[67] Herman Dooyeweerd, *Verniewing en Bezinning om het Reformatorische Grondmotief* (J. B. Van den Brink & Co., 1959), 179.

[68] Dooyeweerd, *Verniewing en Bezinning,* 227: "Het was de historische school, die de valse opvatting heeft verbreid, dat het burgerlijk recht in wezen volksrecht is, en daarmede de baan effende voor het nationaal-socialisme met zijn 'volkse' ideologie."

later Presuppositionalists. One of the core distinctions of Presuppositionalist Traditionalism is its appreciation for the rightful place of a particularist element of epistemology alongside the universalist element. The contemporary interest in the works of Hoedemaker, can, I believe, lead to a renewed reappraisal of Presuppositionalist Traditionalism as an alternative view that can help challenge the dichotomy that is all too characteristic of contemporary debates dominated by the Thomist and Van Tillian schools.

Fact and Historical Revelation

By P. J. Hoedemaker

Translator's Preface

The work translated here was originally published in Dutch as two articles in the nineteenth-century Dutch Anti-Revolutionary journal, *Christelijke Stemmen (Christian Voices)*, during its twenty-fifth year of publication in March 1871.[69] The journal had been established in the 1840s due to a break in the Dutch Réveil. The Réveil was one of three prominent distinguishable theological currents within Dutch Protestantism which emerged as a result of the ecclesiastical disputes in the 1830s, and one which essentially formed the middle party between the liberal Groningen school of Theology and the so-called *Afgescheidenen* or *Separatists*, which split from the established Dutch Reformed Church to form two new denominations, the *Christian Separated Congregations* and the *Reformed Churches under the Cross*.[70] The split was the result of the emergence of

---

[69] The original Dutch title of the articles was "Feit en de geschiedenis der Openbaring." The original Dutch text can be accessed online at https://www.digibron.nl/viewer/ collectie/Digibron/id/tag:Brochures-(SGP),18710501:news ml_6d01f757-50b4-4096-90cd-c341d8700414.

[70] Jasper Vree, "Het Réveil als partij in de Nederlandse samenleving: opkomst, groei, doorwerking en geschiedschrijving (1833–1891)," in *Opwekking van de natie: Het protestantse Réveil in Nederland*, ed. Fred van Lieburg (Verloren, 2012), 63.

liberalism within the Dutch Reformed Church which opposed the doctrinal authority of the traditional Dutch Reformed confessional standards, namely the Belgic Confession (1561), the Heidelberg Catechism (1563) and the Canons of Dordt (1619), known collectively as the Three Forms of Unity.[71] The Réveil sympathized with the theological orthodoxy of the Separatists, but preferred to stay within the structures of the national church.[72] This preference was, importantly, not only based on pragmatic considerations. The men of the Réveil had serious objections to the formation of the new denomination and in particular its implications for Dutch nationhood. They regarded the national church as an important moral compass to the Dutch nation and to the government. They also criticized the separatists' request to the government for civil authorization as a concession to state absolutism, while they, in contradistinction, maintained that the state does not have the right to exercise authority over the church, but only alongside and in cooperation with the church under God's Law.[73] The main difference between the two camps lay in their respective interpretations of Article 28 of the Belgic Confession, which teaches that "all people are obliged" to join as members of the true church: whereas the separatists regarded it as their duty to separate from what they perceived to be a doctrinally false church, the men of the Réveil considered the national church, as historically

---

[71] Harry van Dyke, *Groen van Prinsterer's Lectures in Unbelief and Revolution* (Wedge, 1989), 18–19.

[72] Maartje Janse, "Vereeniging en verlangen om vereenigd te werken—Réveil en civil society," in *Opwekking van de natie: Het protestantse Réveil in Nederland*, ed. Fred van Lieburg (Verloren, 2012), 181.

[73] Groen van Prinsterer, *Gedachten*, 292–93.

legitimate and established, to be the true Dutch church.[74]

However, the Dutch Réveil was much more than merely an ecclesiastical movement. It formed part of a broader, pan-European Reformed revival movement at the time, which emphasized not only personal regeneration and personal experience as central to the Christian faith, but also the idea that religious principles necessarily have socio-political consequences.[75] The movement was therefore committed to the idea that the Kingdom of Christ encompassed every sphere of life.[76]

It was with regard to this central characteristic principle of the Réveil that the aforementioned split within the Dutch branch of the movement occurred during the 1840s. The movement split according to two wings which emerged within it at the time, namely the juridical-confessional wing, which was composed primarily by members in and around Amsterdam, and the ethical-irenic wing, based around Utrecht. The ethical-irenic wing found the emphasis on political party-formation as well as the strict interpretation of the Reformed confessional standards of the juridical-confessional wing highly problematic. With the split, each group, however, started their own publication. The representatives of the ethical-irenic wing started the publication *Ernst en Vrede (Severity and Peace)*, while the juridical-confessional wing founded *Christian Voices*.[77]

---

[74] Rolf Bremmer, "Historische aspecten van de Afscheiding," in *Aspecten van de Afscheiding*, edited by A. de Groot and P. Schram (Wever, 1984), 27–28.

[75] Willem Aalders, *Revolutie en Réveil 1789–1989* (J. N. Voorhove, 1989), 77–79.

[76] Janse, *Vereeniging*, 169.

[77] Elizabeth Kluit, *Het Réveil in Nederland: 1817–1854* (II. J. Paris, 1937), 281, 290.

Hoedemaker was merely a toddler when this split occurred. On top of that, he had moved to Michigan when he was only thirteen years of age. However, upon returning to the Netherlands in 1861, he clearly sided with the juridical-confessional wing of the Réveil and published frequently in *Christian Voices*.[78]

Hoedemaker's two articles in *Christian Voices* translated here were also published as a booklet under the same title later that same year. It is the Dutch philosopher-theologian's clearest and most concise outline of his philosophy of Revelation, and the reader will find it less cumbersome than some of his lengthier works. Because of its concise and specific character, I believe that a broad audience of readers will find it both easily digestible and exceptionally relevant for our twenty-first-century context. For the sake of clarity and context, I have provided this translation with an annotation aimed at elucidating not only historical references and their historical context but also expanding upon the meaning and intention of the text where needed. Wherever Hoedemaker quotes from Scripture, I did not merely translate the literal Dutch text, but rather employed the New King James version of the English Bible.

The historical context of the work itself is evident from the introduction, in which Hoedemaker makes clear his intention to polemicize against the higher critics of the nineteenth century. However, this in itself does not reduce the work to irrelevance for the twenty-first-century reader. On the contrary, the rejection of the supernatural nature of the inspiration of the Bible remains perpetually relevant to all Christians, regardless of their time or context. Furthermore, the work's primary concern is not the doctrine of inspiration itself, but rather the doctrine of Revelation in general, which pertains to the very nature of

---

[78] Mart-Jan Paul, "Hoedemaker en de uitleg van de bijbel," in *Hoedemaker herdacht*, ed. G. Abma and J. de Bruijn (Ten Have, 1989), 116.

human knowledge, for which Scripture does indeed provide the epistemic framework but, but of course includes knowledge acquired by means of general Revelation. One aspect of Hoedemaker's philosophy of Revelation that might come across as strange to some Christians, depending on their confessional tradition, is his emphasis of the historical nature thereof. In passages where this is emphasized I have provided annotations placing them within the context of Hoedemaker's narrative view of Revelation as historically mediated—the view explained in the introduction of this book.

The work in itself furthermore provides a valuable addition to the existing body of Hoedemaker's work translated into English. Recent translations by Ruben Alvarado, published under the titles *The Church and Modern Constitutional Law* (Pantokrator Press, 2014), *Article 36 of the Belgic Confession vindicated against Dr. Abraham Kuyper* (Pantokrator Press, 2019), *Reformed Ecclesiology in an Age of Denominationalism* (Pantokrator Press, 2019), and *The Politics of Antithesis: The Antirevolutionary Government of Abraham Kuyper 1901–1905* (Pantokrator Press, 2021), are a testimony to the increased interest in the work of Hoedemaker. That such a host of translations of Hoedemaker's works would appear more than a century after his death, is in itself a testimony to the continuing relevance of this great Dutch Reformed philosopher and theologian for contemporary discussions in philosophy, theology, and politics in the tumultuous time we currently find ourselves in.

It is my sincere hope that Hoedemaker's philosophy of Revelation as it comes to light in this extraordinary and sadly, too often neglected contribution of his, will aid the reader in coming to a greater understanding of and appreciation for the nature of human knowledge as essentially the Revelation of the facts of reality revealed by the Creator of that reality, the Triune God.

Jan Adriaan Schlebusch

PART ONE

Revelation as Historical Fact

In the second edition of the journal *Theological Studies and Criticism*[79] we find a letter by Friedrich Schleiermacher[80] which he had written to his friend and younger contemporary Lücke,[81] in which the following passage can be found:

> If I am not mistaken, then we will have to sacrifice much of what the masses has always regarded to be integral to Christianity.

---

[79] *Theologische Studien und Kritiken* was a liberal theological journal published during the nineteenth and early twentieth centuries in Germany. The second edition of this journal was published in 1829, forty-one years before Hoedemaker wrote this work.

[80] Friedrich Schleiermacher (1768–1834) was a liberal German theologian who is widely known as the father of modern hermeneutics and higher criticism, a naturalistic approach to the Bible which subjects its authority to human reason. See Theodore Vial, *Schleiermacher: A Guide for the Perplexed* (Bloomsbury, 2013), 4.

[81] Friedrich Lücke was a fellow higher critic and editor of Schleiermacher's collected works. See Andrew Kloes, *The German Awakening: Protestant Renewal After the Enlightenment, 1815–1848* (Oxford University Press, 2019), 265.

Without even getting into the issue of a six-day creation, how long do you think the very doctrine of creation itself can be upheld against a worldview built upon scientific principles which none in due course can ignore? How long will it be, until faith in the miracles of the New Testament, not even to mention those of the Old Testament, would have to be discarded for the arguments of a more scientific approach which disregards the supernatural nature of Revelation? Personally, I do not expect to see this happen in my lifetime, and I will lay down my head in peace. But you, however, my, friend, you and the men of your generation, must know what to do when such a time comes. Would you then still side yourself with Christianity and allow yourself to be beleaguered by science? You would be bombarded by mockery. And even if this doesn't bother you, consider that you would become completely isolated from society if you were to continue to try and uphold the orthodoxy of the faith against unbelief. That would indeed be the great end result of the development of world history, that science would ally itself with unbelief, while Christianity and Barbarism would hereafter be inseparable.[82]

---

[82] In this quote, Schleiermacher expresses a very typical Enlightenment or liberal view of world history, which at the time was commonly thought of as culminating in an ideal universal human society based upon humanity itself as ultimate epistemic and moral standard, an idea expressed for example in Immanuel Kant's *Die Religion innerhalb der Grenzen der blossen Vernunft* (Nicolovius, 1793), 88–92. This work was translated into English as *Religion within the Boundaries of Mere Reason*.

Such was the prophecy of Schleiermacher. Has it been fulfilled, or will it be fulfilled in future? Consider that it has already been forty years since he had written this and that not only he but also Lücke and even some of the younger generation of critical scholars have now already been buried. In the meantime, the Church and a notable number of its scholars still maintain those doctrines which Schleiermacher regarded as "beleaguered by science," which would tend to make one believe that the danger he had foreseen is by now already something of the past. However, when we consider other signs of the times, including how unbelief now characterizes most scholarship on the doctrinc of Revelation, and how among this generation those who follow the spirit of the age far outnumber the defenders of faith in Divine Revelation, as well as to what extent the former is better equipped and far more vocal, then we could still rightly fear a time in the near future when ignorance alone would be employed in defense of the authority of Revelation.

While we don't want to simply ignore this very real and disturbing phenomenon of our times, we can take courage in the assurance that Schleiermacher's prophecy had not only remained unfulfilled until now, but that it will always remain unfulfilled. And this assurance is not only derived from Holy Scripture and our own experience. In fact, it largely rests upon the knowledge that all truth is from God and that He is Lord even over the sphere of science.[83] It also rests not only upon the knowledge that whenever and wherever heresy manifests itself, it takes on a self-destructive nature as soon as it positions itself in opposition to truth, but also on the conviction that all the true

---

[83] Our knowledge that God is sovereign even over the sciences is of course itself derived from Divine Revelation in Scripture: see, e.g., Romans 11:36, Ephesians 1:11, 2 Corinthians 10:5, Colossians 1:16, and Revelation 4:11.

findings of science, even inasmuch as it attempts to promote unbelief, would necessarily always be in accordance with the principles of faith—principles which has been confirmed by all of history.[84]

The words spoken to Ahab when the Syrians claimed that the gods of Israel are mountain gods and would not be able to hold their own against Syrian gods during a battle in a valley, remains ever-true: "Thus says the LORD: 'Because the Syrians have said, "The LORD is God of the hills, but He is not God of the valleys," therefore I will deliver all this great multitude into your hand, and you shall know that I am the LORD.'"[85]

Schleiermacher had descended into a fatal heresy, through which he separated that which God has unified—science and faith. It is in light of this heresy that his prophecy needs to be understood. This prophecy will remain an embarrassment as long as we maintain that science and faith can not only be harmonized, but are in fact inseparable.[86]

---

[84] Bavinck likewise notes that no knowledge which does not proceed from faith in God can lay claim to be truthful, since "truth can only be attributed to knowledge which proceeds from faith. Faith is the means of acquiring knowledge ... Faith and science therefore stand in the same relation to each other as conception and birth, tree and fruits, work and wages: knowledge is the fruit and wages of faith" (Bavinck, *Christelijke Wetenschap*, 15–16).

[85] 1 Kings 20:28.

[86] Hoedemaker rightly argues for the superiority of Christian science. This same argument can be found in the work of his contemporary from across the Atlantic, Robert Lewis Dabney, who, in a sermon of the following year, also noted that "I hold that there is, there can be, no proper collision between the most explicit and authoritative theistic testimony and sound natural science." Robert Lewis Dabney, "A Caution against Anti-Christian Science: A Sermon Preached in the Synod of Virginia, October 20, 1871," in *Discussions, Volume III: Philosophical* (Ross House, 1980), 134.

In this regard we must make a distinction between that science which is in a temporary and unholy alliance with unbelief and science as it truly is: a servant of truth, whether that be consciously or unconsciously.[87] For as long as it is made subservient to heresy, science destroys itself, while in service of faith it comes to true fruition.[88]

And if you desire proof of this, it can be clearly seen in the history of the past several decades. One system of science promptly replaces another, so much so that we cannot but echo the complaint of the prophet Joel: "What the chewing locust left, the swarming locust has eaten; What the swarming locust left, the crawling locust has eaten; And what the crawling locust left, the consuming locust has eaten."[89] In our own context it can be said that what deism left, rationalism has destroyed; what rationalism has left, pantheism has destroyed; whatever has been left untouched by pantheism, has been consumed by empiricism; and that which has not been destroyed by

---

[87] Bavinck would later likewise argue that science necessarily proceeds, "either willingly or unwillingly," from "the acknowledgment of the existence of truth, goodness and beauty which cannot be deduced from empirical realities" (Bavinck, *Christelijke Wetenschap*, 72).

[88] Hoedemaker's argument here is fundamentally what is commonly described as Presuppositionalist, that is, based on the conviction that the truth of the Christian religion provides the only solid framework for rational thought. This exact sentiment was echoed later by the great Dutch-American apologist Cornelius van Til, who argued that by setting up himself as the standard of truth, man destroys the possibility of truth altogether, because, since because God has created everything, "not one single fact in the universe can be known truly by man without the existence of God." Cornelius Van Til, *Introduction to Systematic Theology*, Second Edition (Presbyterian and Reformed Publishing, 1974), 36.

[89] Joel 1:4.

empiricism, has come under fire from materialism. Each of these systems are marked by their aversion of Christianity, but nonetheless, they can never be said to have destroyed Christianity, because one can never destroy truth as such, only deny it to yourself. These systems act in the name of science, and each of them, on various grounds, place themselves in opposition to Christianity. And what has been the consequence of this? That each has superseded and neutralized the other. In this regard they are not unlike the men of David and Ishboseth, who slaughtered each other as we read in 2 Samuel 2:16: "And each one grasped his opponent by the head and thrust his sword in his opponent's side; so they fell down together."

In this regard even these anti-Christian systems have been of service to the faith and as I will show later, and they have ended up being most useful in quite a number of ways.

The Swiss people have a beautiful legend regarding the origin of their mountains: a clan of ice giants who had been rejected by their brothers came out of the Himalayas, but because of the long and grueling journey they sought for a resting place but in the process were reduced to a dead ridge. The leaders of the traveling company of ice giants were the Monk, the Virgin, and the Ogre,[90] and their wish seemed granted when they conquered the valleys, drove away its inhabitants and consumed the towns and cities. However, there was a great cry for help from the natives, which was answered by mockery on the part of the giants, but was heard by God in Heaven who is never merely an idle Bystander. Through the thunder the Lord's voice could be heard: "Unto here you shall go, but no further!" And consequently, these giants

---

[90] These are the names of the three highest summits of the Bernese Alps, located in western Switzerland.

were robbed of their lives and became the bulwark of a free Switzerland.

So it has been and so it will always be with those sciences, facts, and concepts which, having previously depended upon the protection of Divine Revelation, neglected their duty of gratefulness by now positioning themselves against that very Revelation in attempting to suppress it. They will, like the ice giants, only end up being a bulwark around Revelation.

The reader should admit that the Swiss legend is indeed beautiful, but what consolation does it offer in a time when modern science threatens to wholly expel Revelation from its rightful domain, which encompasses all of reality. And what is proposed in its place? Empty phrases and expectations—the kind that can never be fulfilled. Did not liberalism promise us peace and stability on the same grounds as modern science, while at the same time ripping out the ground beneath our feet, leaving nothing to build upon?[91]

---

[91] This is a classic example of a conservative, anti-Enlightenment argument from the nineteenth century. The central argument that characterized the political theory of Hoedemaker's Anti-Revolutionary predecessor, Guillaume Groen van Prinsterer, was that liberalism, in ridding politics from its solid foundation in the belief in the sovereignty of God and replacing it with the sovereignty of man inevitably leads to a kind of anarchy from which centralized government tyranny alone offers liberation. He furthermore expressed the same optimism as Hoedemaker did with regard to the inevitable failure of godless systems, which, because of their complete incompatibility with created reality, cannot be maintained in the long run. Guillaume Groen van Prinsterer, *Ongeloof en Revolutie (1847)*, ed. Roel Kuiper and Arie Kuiper (Nederlands Dagblad, 2008), 389.

This dynamic in the political domain was recognized by Hoedemaker himself, who wrote in his work *Heel de kerk en heel de volk* ("All of the Church and all of the Nation") that "the [French] Revolution has replaced the authority of God with the authority of

What guarantee do we then have that there will ever be an end to the progress currently being made by scientific unbelief? Is it not false to suppose that this very suppression of the faith by godless science will one day be beneficial to Christianity? No, on the contrary: it is vital that we maintain and defend this conviction if we don't want faith to be associated with barbarism on the one hand and that we don't want to be suppressed and deceived by godless science on the other. When the sciences are dominated by unbelief, it becomes more vital for Christians to proactively engage in the sciences, since these two are, after all, inseparable.[92]

It is only natural that the believer is never the first to accept findings which are in opposition to or seem to be in opposition to the Scriptures or the traditional convictions of Christianity. In this regard one could claim that he is "unscientific" in that he does not view the data without any biases or preconceived commitments which are not shared by other scientists. Convictions are, after all, not so easily discarded.[93]

---

man ... this is the seed of oppression ... by which in the name of liberty the greatest evils are committed" (26).

[92] This exact sentiment would be echoed two years after the publication of Hoedemaker's articles by Robert Lewis Dabney, who wrote in his own article published in the Southern Presbyterian Review in 1873, in which he argued that "natural science ... especially geology, have been so largely perverted to the interest of unbelief" that it can really be called nothing more than a "sham-science." Robert Lewis Dabney, "The Caution against anti-Christian science criticized by Dr. Woodrow," *Discussions*, 3:140, 144.

[93] The positivist idea of "objective" scientific research has largely been discarded since the dawn of the twentieth century. In this regard the Christian philosopher Herman Dooyeweerd (1894–1977) did immensely important work in showing how any and all scientific research is inescapably dependent upon presuppositions or pre-theoretical commitments on the part of the researcher. In other

However, in the long run the believer cannot simply turn a blind eye to the findings of scientific research. He must take into account the findings of positivist research, and in fact can do so without fear because he believes that truth is of God and that all truths, whether it be scientific or theological, are interrelated, even in cases where he is not immediately able to provide an adequate solution to apparent contradictions. With that very conviction he proceeds to continue with his research. And afterward it will become apparent that those findings for which he had not at first accounted in his system, only enabled him to more fully understand the meaning of Holy Scripture.[94]

---

words, pre-theory is a prerequisite for theory, and even the natural science is itself dependent upon certain theological presuppositions which are accepted on faith in order to become at all possible; see Herman Dooyeweerd, *Der crisis der humanistische staatsleer in het licht eener calvinistische kosmologie en kennistheorie* (Ten Have, 1931), 90. The idea that non-Christian scientific researchers can any more claim "objectivity" than Christian scientific research is based upon nineteenth-century propaganda that should have, at the time, been more thoroughly refuted than Hoedemaker does here. Today the existence of a philosophy of science and even a philosophy of mathematics are widely recognized by scholars, who know that presuppositional convictions are required to enable any scientific research at all.

[94] While there is certainly room for, on certain matters, adapting our understanding of Holy Scripture in light of the evidences of natural science, we must be very careful not to do so at the cost of the authority of Scripture itself. One example of where this has been wrongly done in the past, is e.g. through the theory of Old Earth Creationism—an attempt to reconcile the Biblical account of creation with unbelieving scientists' findings through radiocarbon dating. This attempt fails, however, in light of texts such as Exodus 20:11, which expressly teaches that God created the earth within the six days described in Genesis 1. Rather than accepting the findings

It was after all the findings which seemed to contradict the calculations of astronomers which enabled Le Verrier[95] to discover the unknown cause of the disruption of the courses of several stars and through which he discovered a new planet, Neptune. And yet, even if it could then be shown that these new

---

of research which claims that the earth is millions of years old, we must challenge the presuppositions of uniformitarianism or gradualism underlying that research, by showing that the existence of a Creator, the very foundation enabling scientific research, actually invalidates uniformitarianism (and its geological variant gradualism) and necessitates catastrophism, since only such a model allows for the intervention of a divine agent in natural history. Uniformitarianism is a pre-scientific assumption that the same natural laws and processes which operate in the universe today has always operated in the same way in the past. The fact that leading philosophers of science today recognize this presupposition, which itself cannot be scientifically proven, as central to geologic investigation, is evidence of the blatant false atheistic assumptions behind evolutionary theory. See Robert Stern and Taras Gerya, "Earth, Evolution, Emergence and Uniformitarianism," *GSA Today* 31, no. 1 (2021): 32–33. Faith in the existence of a sovereign God as Creator, on the contrary, necessitates presupposing catastrophism, the idea that the earth (and the universe) has been largely formed by sudden events of a universal scope. The very acceptance of catastrophism, necessitated by theism, invalidates the findings of all research which claims that the earth has to be millions or billions of years old, as such research is founded upon a false presupposition.

In this light Dabney also rightly accuses positivism of wrongly holding that "all logical principles are empirical... [seeking] to find all the sources of cognition in the senses. This common error characterized the deadly philosophy of Hume, the scheme of Auguste Comte, termed by himself *positivism*, and the somewhat diverse systems of Buckle, John Stuart Mill, and of Darwin and Huxley...and consequently reach, more or less fully, the result of blank materialism" (Dabney, *Dr. Woodrow*, 142–43).

95 The French astronomer Urbain Joseph Le Verrier (1811–77).

findings did not confirm the traditional principles of astronomy, then this science would thereby still not have lost its credibility, since astronomy is not dependent upon the theories of either Ptolemy, Kepler, or Newton.

It is not any different in theology than it is in natural science—inexplicable phenomena help us grow in our knowledge of her grow even more. After all, Divine Revelation itself cannot be held responsible for whatever is rightly or wrongly derived from it. The facts of Revelation stand above the interpretation thereof, as it stands above derived systems and faith stands above theory.

We have indeed discarded much of what we had previously regarded as the implications of Christianity, and in this regard Schleiermacher had a point. However, he failed to recognize that we have discovered so much more in an even more refined form.

Nonetheless, that the findings of science have made the faithful reconsider some of their previous assumptions is a well-known fact. We are now faced with new issues and fight with new weapons. A man who has overslept for many years just like Rip van Winkle in Washington Irving's legend would not be immediately informed regarding the nature of his new context, but it would take him some time to fully grasp it.[96]

Consider the various contentious issues of the past several decades, which we have ceased to consider as such. Think, for example, of the question regarding the literal inspiration of Scripture. We have not compromised this principle by any means, and yet the fight regarding Biblical inspiration currently focuses

---

[96] Irving's short story, published in 1819, is a tale about a Dutch-American named Rip van Winkle who, after consuming a mysterious liquor, falls asleep for twenty years.

on the issue of whether we currently possess something which can be called Revelation at all. Our opponents have, in fact, shifted their position and we have been forced back in our defense of the authority of Scripture to the defense of the very existence of Revelation as such. And this shift should be seen not as a loss to the faith, but as a gain. The very enemy which has sought to drive us back, has, in actual fact, done us a great service—greater than they could have ever imagined. Because now we have been forced to develop an even clearer and more thorough theology of Revelation.[97]

In Greek mythology we find the story of Antaeus, the son of Neptune and Terra (the earth) who fought with Hercules, who threw him to the earth time and again, only for him to each time gain renewed strength from his mother. As such he remained unbeatable until Hercules finally held on to him and squeezed him to death at his chest.

Antaeus is a symbol of the Christian faith. It remains invincible as long as we have the firm foundation of the facts of Revelation, which has birthed it, to stand upon. The Hercules of science continually hurls the faith back to these facts, but by means of such attacks the faith only goes from strength to strength. Only if and when we forsake the solid

---

[97] Hoedemaker here makes a very important point that is equally applicable to all contexts. One recent example is how the forced closure of churches enforced by the Covid-19 lockdowns imposed by governments—a clear violation of the religious rights of Christians—have helped the Church to more thoroughly develop doctrines regarding the nature and limits of medical mandates and civil government as well as the nature and essence of worship services. This more thoroughly developed and increasingly rigorous theology is manifested, for example, in the now-famous Warrenton Declaration *on Medical Mandates, Biblical Ethics and Authority* (2021).

ground of Revelation, as well as that of experience, so that we are carried away by mere speculation, it loses its strength and identity.[98]

But understand me well: I do not claim that facts and theories on the one hand or doctrines on the other can be separated or that we are in a position to make a choice between one or the other. They cannot be separated, but may only be distinguished. The battles of recent years have taught us the exact kind of relationship in which the two stand to each other and this is a lesson we should never forget. Doctrine is derived from and rests upon fact, upon which it stands or falls. We have been forced to re-investigate the facts of Revelation, but only to acquire a better understanding and launch a better defense of true doctrine. In times past there have been numerous doctrinal disputes, but we are now well on our way to seeing all these doctrines unified as parts of the whole. The true divinity and humanity of Jesus, his mediatorship, the Person and the work of the Holy Spirit—all of these have become clearer through time as will the fact that one has to accept these truths when one accepts the resurrection and any miracles recorded in Revelation.

We have precisely that science which so often allies itself with unbelief and apostasy to thank for the fact that we see so many things so much more clearly now. It has liberated us from our own chains and

---

[98] Hoedemaker's epistemic reliance upon Scripture and experience (or history) is typical for nineteenth-century Christian conservatism. For Hoedemaker's predecessor, Guillaume Groen van Prinsterer, e.g., history's authority is always tied to its proximate relationship to God's creative-redemptive order and purpose for the cosmos as revealed in Scripture: that is, tied to its cosmological genesis in terms of its divine design, as well as its cosmological telos in the glorification of Jesus Christ (Groen van Prinsterer, *Ongeloof en Revolutie*, 57, 76–77, 243).

nudged us along on the path to better expositions of doctrines, and now we can fearlessly repel all attacks that very science launches against us.

Regardless of what science may take from us, it can never take away the fact of Revelation, and the truth of all its content. Apart from this, there is room for re-evaluation in light of scientific findings, even with regard to that which we may have previously wrongly regarded as absolutely integral to Christianity.

Moderns claim that there is no natural knowledge of God which can be scientifically studied. It has therefore disputed what among Christians are widely accepted claims regarding the additional proofs of God's existence, and which we have long held to be irrefutable. It has expelled from scientific discourse all mention of the immortality of the soul. It has re-evaluated all the long-held moral principles, where some have even declared liberty itself to be an illusion. In the place of general Revelation it proposes an endless skepticism, wherein all that is beautiful and dear to us merely sinks away.

This science thus opposes faith in Divine Revelation on the basis of rationalism, which denies necessity of special Revelation and holds nature to be sufficient. But this opposition ended up being not unlike the classical example of Plutarch where a certain boy tried to hit his dog with a stone but accidentally struck his stepmother, after which he mumbled that "the throw was not in vain." It is far from me to attribute such complacency to modern science, but this changes nothing with regard to the facts of the matter. Rationalism has aimed its stone to faith in Divine Revelation, but ended up only causing destruction to liberal theology, and thus "the throw was not in vain."[99]

---

[99] This phenomenon, namely that it is the counterfeit religion of "liberal Christianity" that suffers the hardest blows from the attacks

This purely negative proposition of modern science, namely that it recognizes no natural Revelation or knowledge of God, is not at odds with what we believe. It must merely be countered by adding that this can only be true inasmuch as the facts, through which God reveals his work, do not make themselves known.

Our faith in Revelation also rests upon a historical foundation. We do not derive nor test the facts to science per se, since it is not equipped to teach us anything about the supernatural and therefore holds no authority in this regard.[100] Rather, we employ the principles, methods, and results of scientific investigation as a means of elucidating irrefutable and

---

of secular scientists while orthodox or Biblical Christianity has remained steadfast, has been confirmed ever since Hoedemaker wrote this in 1871. In the twenty-first century there is now virtually nothing left of what had been known as liberal theology in Hoedemaker's day. The failure of liberal theology has become increasingly evident ever since the Second World War, so much so that the enemies of the faith, in the form of Cultural Marxism, have now turned their attention wholly to the more conservative denominations in an attempt to fight Christianity through subversion. See Paul Weyrich and William Lind, *The Next Conservatism* (St. Augustine's Press, 2009), 36.

[100] Hoedemaker explains what he means by this in the following paragraph. Since science only studies natural phenomena, scientific investigation is limited to the study of secondary or natural causes of such phenomena, and is in need of Divine Revelation for enlightening its findings with regard to the supernatural First Cause of all the phenomena that it studies, namely God. Dabney likewise notes that "it is the business and the boast of physical science to resolve as many effects as possible into their second causes. Repeated and fascinating success in these solutions gradually amount to a temptation to the mind to look less for the great First Cause. The experience of thousands, who were not watchful and prayerful, has proved this" (Dabney, *Dr. Woodrow*, 146).

indispensable truths regarding the supernatural. We do not believe that in the long run there will be any conflict between science and faith.

It is not our theology, but rather liberal theology which has separated itself from science and placed itself in opposition against it. After all, if it is true that science only teaches us about natural or secondary causes, and the findings of scientific inquiry is regarded by liberal theology as all-encompassing, then it follows that the "faith" and "religion" it promotes, must stand in stark opposition to what it considers to be "science."

In the realm of secondary causes there is, of course, no room for a divine Agent, unless one were to pantheistically identify Him with nature itself and describe Him with the inscription that was found above the entrance of the temple of Isis in Egypt: "I am everything that was, that is and that will be. No one can lift my veil." But we deny that there are any merits to such a system and it cannot be considered true religion. Alternatively, if one were to escape such a system by placing God at the very end of a long series of natural causes and consequences, that any knowledge of Him, love toward Him or relationship with Him would become wholly impossible. Like Rousseau, who once lamented that "there are so many people between me and God," we would then also lament: "There are so many causes between me and God."[101] We would not regard such a religion to be scientific.

---

[101] Jean-Jacques Rousseau (1712–78) was a liberal French philosopher. He is best known for his social contract theory, which is widely regarded as the foundation of modern liberal democracy; see Milan Zafirovsky, *The Enlightenment and its Effects on Modern Society* (Springer, 2011), 85. For Rousseau, every individual, in his natural state, is truly free, uncorrupted, and absolutely sovereign. For him, individual liberty and sovereignty entail egocentric self-

Beets[102] once described modern liberal theology accurately in one of his poems, in which he attributes to it the following words:

> Cause and consequence keep all things in order,
> Consequences become causes,
> Causes Consequences,
> It is a system of loops and links,
> Unbreakable, regardless what one thinks,
> Through it the things on earth can be explained,
> So that no uncertainty can further be entertained.

There may be scientists found among modern or liberal Christians, but their theology is thoroughly unscientific. If the prophecy of Schleiermacher can be considered to have found any fulfillment at all, it would be in liberal "Christianity," since she is not only cut off from science, but her doctrine of God is immensely limited by her attempt to incorporate Him in a finite series of natural causes. This religion is nothing more than a Fata Morgana,[103] a visual deception and a reflection of a religious life attempting to circumvent the true sources of Revelation, and one

---

servitude free from any constraints. Jean-Jacques Rousseau, *Du contrat social, ou, Principes du droit politique* (M. M. Rey, 1762), 69. It is in light of Rousseau's anti-Christian philosophy, and his consequent opposition to the Church, that the quotation here referenced by Hoedemaker should be understood.

[102] Nicolaas Beets (1814–1903) was a Dutch Reformed minister and poet. He was a prominent and highly influential figure in Anti-Revolutionary (conservative) circles in the Netherlands during the nineteenth century.

[103] A mirage. "Fata Morgana," the term Hoedemaker here uses for mirage, is derived from the well-known and commonly used Italian name for the sorceress Morgan the Fairy in Arthurian legend. The term became common usage due to the belief that mirages could be the result of witchcraft.

merely trying to fulfill the natural spiritual desires of the human heart.

Since the challenges of unbelieving scholars have therefore forced us back into defending our recognition of the very fact of Revelation, it has placed us before a further challenge, since we were now forced into making a distinction between Revelation and Scripture, that is, between content and form. Again, it was "science," which, in service of unbelief, forced us thereunto.

Nonetheless, Scripture is formally and intrinsically connected with Revelation as its certificate, so to speak. Not only do divine acts and divine words clarify each other, but we also have the record of divine acts recorded in Scripture. Revelation manifests itself in Scripture and came to us in this form. But we must never forget that the Word became Flesh prior to the closing of the canon of Scripture, and that He would eternally remain even after Scripture has passed. People have accused us of Bibliolatry, that is, of an exaggerated and superstitious glorification of the Bible. But this accusation lacks any merit.[104]

But still, over against the shallow position of rationalism, namely that the Word of God is only contained in Scripture, the Church has always confessed that all of Scripture is in fact God's Word. This doctrine of Scripture has always been maintained and should continue to be maintained if we want to maintain the objective character of Revelation over against the heresy that it is the word of man, which can always be subjected to mere human theories and insights.[105]

---

[104] Hoedemaker here places the historical Revelation of Jesus Christ in the flesh on par with the written Word of God as a form of special and infallible Revelation.

[105] Hoedemaker here evidently makes an argument for what is known as the doctrine of the plenary inspiration of Scripture, i.e.,

On the other hand, much has changed over the past few decades thanks to this very battle. We have learned to make a distinction, albeit no separation, between Revelation and its form. The relationship between the two has been turned upside down. Our faith in Revelation therefore does not rest upon a theory, which we have derived from Holy Scripture.[106] Our defense of the form no longer rests upon an anxious clinging to the letter, even though we have by no

---

that every word of Scripture is fully inspired by God the Holy Spirit and that the Bible is therefore infallible in all matters that it addresses. For Hoedemaker, Scripture not merely *contains* the Word of God, as if some parts thereof could be deemed fallible, but all of Scripture *is* the Word of God. Philippus Jacobus Hoedemaker, *De Mozaïsche oorsprong der wetten in de boeken Exodus, Leviticus en Numeri: lezingen over de moderne Schriftkritiek des Ouden Testaments* (Daamen, 1895), 35.

[106] Hoedemaker here argues against a mechanical view of divine inspiration of Scripture, that is, the idea that Scripture came down from heaven as an abstraction apart from redemptive history, by noting that Revelation is always historically mediated. This also underlies his emphasis on the distinction between content and form. While this is true and an important fact of Revelation, it remains uncertain who he is polemicizing against, as the mechanical view of inspiration has never been widely held among Christian theologians—not in Hoedemaker's time, not in the history of the Church preceding him, and not by successors. Throughout his argument he also makes statements such as that Divine Revelation is "not limited or dependent upon the existence of Scripture" because Christ was historically revealed in the flesh and God's sovereignty is revealed throughout history. While this is true, it seems as though he does fail to articulate the uniqueness of that special Revelation which we have received in the form of Scripture by neglecting to mention that without it, we would not only not be able to acquire sufficient knowledge of Christ in order to obtain salvation, but we would also not learn God's will sufficiently for the purpose of serving Him aright in this life.

means compromised the letter. The battle now pertains to the overarching principles. Strauss, in his preface to his work on dogmatics, claimed that "the doctrine of literal inspiration is the Achilles heel of orthodoxy."[107] We thank him for showing us where the enemy focuses its attacks and will make sure not to expose ourselves unnecessarily to the arrows of higher criticism.

Revelation is a fact. It is a historical fact, and it is one that continues throughout history. It is not merely limited to the past. No, it has been mediated to us through history. We look back upon the history of the Christian Church, which itself confirms the truths contained in Holy Scripture, that is, the sacred and redemptive history of Israel, the people who had mediated that Revelation. And precisely because this sacred history bears the distinct mark of divine inspiration and divine guidance it is clearly distinguished from anything ever produced by man. That the truth of Revelation is then confirmed by the flow of history, cannot be denied. Moreover, its flow is everywhere recognizable.[108]

Even if, God forbid, Scripture was to be taken from us, the Revelation of history still remains. Or would you argue that if all the libraries in the Netherlands were to be burned down, the history of the

---

[107] David Friedrich Strauss (1808–74) was, like Schleiermacher, a liberal German theologian.

[108] Hoedemaker is not arguing for an open canon or for the insufficiency of Scripture. His argument here pertains to Revelation as subjectively received by mankind. In other words, while God Himself, the Object of Revelation, is infinite and eternal, and His infallible Revelation as recorded in His Word is set, this Revelation is subjectively received by mankind throughout history by virtue of the never-ending work of His Holy Spirit in the hearts and minds of people, whereby the knowledge of God is continually increasing throughout history (Habakkuk 2:14).

Reformation and our war with Spain would not still be written in our towns and cities, in our churches and monasteries, in our customs, our laws, and our language? Or do you believe that if all the books on geology were to be destroyed, the sediments and fossils would not be preserved by the calendars of creation?

Therefore, the fact of Revelation is not limited or dependent upon the existence of Holy Scripture, because this fact manifests itself in creation, in experience, and in the history of nations.[109]

It is thanks to science, and thanks to its battle against the faith, that we have come to recognize this fact. It has, unintentionally, emancipated us from the slavery which we had brought upon ourselves. Now we are willing to test everything that it claims regarding Holy Scripture, since our faith rests upon the foundation of the fact of Revelation and the history of Revelation. This fact is of course nothing new. It has been recognized throughout history, but in recent times we have been guided to a renewed appreciation thereof.

---

[109] This statement is technically true, but again, it seems as if Hoedemaker here again fails to articulate the qualitative difference between special and general Revelation in terms of their ability to communicate the will of God and salvific truths with clarity and sufficiency. What is particularly noteworthy, however, is the fact that the influence of the Historical School is quite evident on his thought in that he repeatedly equates general Revelation with history as opposed to nature.

PART TWO

The Scope and Authority of Revelation

If Revelation is a fact, then it is not merely the mechanism by which the divine authority of the writings of apostles or prophets are elevated above scrutiny, but it is the inescapable reality in which God reveals Himself, if He desires to make Himself personally known to us as He exists independently of His creation.

The resistance of science against the idea of supernatural Revelation has amplified the true wonder behind the fact of Revelation. It has also shown us that the findings of science cannot be viewed independently of faith.[110] The mere fact of Revelation is itself sufficient to defend and justify the Christian faith in the court of science.

Unbelieving naturalists do not allow for attributing supernatural phenomena to divine intervention. According to them this hampers

---

[110] God is the creator of the universe and consequently also of all of the scientific facts contained in that universe. The word "fact" itself is derived from the Latin word *facere*, which means "to create." Scientific facts, therefore, ultimately derive both their existence and their meaning from their Creator.

scientific investigation. But they are confusing the pagan concept of supernatural with the Christian concept thereof. The facts of Revelation aren't merely unfathomable phenomena in nature, of which the witness declares "I cannot understand it." On the contrary, it is God who establishes the facts, and makes Himself and His will known to us thereby. It serves as understandable signs and symbols of God's will. Revelation itself, after all, entails revealing something! Therefore, rest assured: the Christian faith can never serve to justify ignorance or opposition to scientific progress.[111]

But, these scientists continue, we surely then cannot allow for the possibility of the disruption of natural laws and processes, which would be the inevitable consequence of divine intervention in nature. These laws in themselves are, after all, revealed by God.[112]

But then I rest my case, because the wonder of Revelation proposes just this: that there is Someone who reveals Himself through the facts; something other than a mere natural force, and therefore Someone transcending nature, namely a personal God. The wonder and reality of Revelation is not in opposition to the laws of nature, but neither is it a product of a natural force. To determine, in each

---

[111] This is because all scientific progress is dependent upon the Revelation of scientific facts by God, since man cannot know anything about anything if it is not revealed to him by God.

[112] The argument to which Hoedemaker responds here is rooted in a form of deism, which entails a strict separation of divine works of creation from divine works of providence and redemption. It is a pagan idea with no place in Christian theology. The same God who created the universe, after all, actively rules over that universe, and is consequently free to engage in and providentially direct it, at any time, even without the use of those natural laws and processes which He normally employs as the secondary means of providence.

particular instance, whether God works in or with nature or not, we leave up to you. From our perspective, we do not desire the fact of Revelation to be separated from nature, for in reality it cannot. If you were to ask us then in what way God reveals Himself personally in nature, our answer is this: He reveals Himself as its Creator and Sustainer, and as such He is free to create something new, to work through natural forces unknown to us, or through unknown combinations of known forces, in order to reveal Himself. In no way is the natural order anymore disrupted hereby as it would be when I hold a rock in my hand which would have otherwise fallen to the ground. In such a case my personal power would not only work with natural forces, but in accordance with it.[113] Yet the energy required of me to hold up the rock stands in direct relation to the impact of the earth's gravity.

The wonder of Revelation therefore lies the fact that God reveals His personal engagement in and with Creation, but this is not the complete sum of the matter, since this very fact presupposes the existence of a history of Revelation.

Miracles and supernatural realities are not merely a set of incoherent facts or events without any relation to each other or to the preordained divine plan for creation, but they stand in a threefold relationship: to nature in which it manifests, to humanity for which it manifests and to the divine purpose of which it manifests.

---

[113] Hoedemaker points to the fact that, since natural laws and processes derive their existence and meaning from God, they are also impossible to understand apart from Him. This in itself points to the superiority of Christian science over non-Christian science, since without the presupposition of an omnipotent Creator-God who sustains creation, there can be no logic behind nor a set order or structure to that creation.

In scientific investigation, the rejection of supernatural elements or forces is maintained for the purpose of eliminating isolated facts which bear no relation to scientific realities. But this amounts to a fatal misunderstanding of the implications of such a rejection. It also entails a rejection of the existence of a moral order, of the destiny and purpose of humanity itself, as well as of the purpose and plan behind all of creation. Allow me to briefly explain why I say this.

There can be nothing found in nature that is wholly new and not preordained. Even the smallest and most insignificant creations inescapably stand in direct relation to their Creator. All creations also stand in relation to each other. They cannot be wholly isolated from each other. There are plants which exhibit characteristics we associate with animals, and there are animals which exhibit plant-like characteristics. In the lower creations we often find a reflection of higher creations. In the rock-layers of Brazil, for example, we also find the same fauna that can be found in its forests and grasslands.

What the apostle Paul had said regarding the Old Testament believers, that they would be incomplete without us, the believers of the New Covenant,[114] is equally applicable to the various species and races found in nature, who are bound together as one divinely-created organic whole.[115]

---

[114] Possibly a reference to Romans 4:23–24 or 1 Corinthians 10:11.

[115] Here we find in Hoedemaker's argument a principle which was, in the twentieth century, more thoroughly and clearly articulated by the American Presbyterian philosopher R. J. Rushdoony, who pointed out how creation reflects the One and the Many characteristic of the Triune God's nature as One God in Three distinct persons: "In the triune God, one God, three persons, there is an equal ultimacy of the one and the many. Unity and particularity are equally important ... The Christian doctrine of the Trinity avoids the pitfalls of the abstract universal (or one) and the abstract

Scientific research has taught us this. In this regard there is truth in Darwin's theory, but this idea is also found in Scripture: in Genesis 3 and Romans 8, in the paradise prior to the Fall, in the retribution for sin, the resurrection of Christ, and the new heavens and the new earth.

Man is the moral head of creation and God is the Head of humanity. The final word in the book of nature is the first word of the Book of Revelation, which reads: "Seth, the son of Adam, Adam, the son of God."[116] When it comes to the origin of man, we necessarily approach the supernatural.[117] Man stands on the border between the animal kingdom and the Kingdom of God. Ask of secular science what the distinction is between man and animal, and you will find no satisfactory answer. When looking at man's design and purpose, our aspirations, our sense of justice, of guilt and of truth, even the imbalance between knowledge and desire found in us, all bear witness to our supernatural origin. Man's supernatural origin also necessitates a supernatural Revelation as a means of gaining any knowledge with

---

particulars, in that neither the universals, or oneness of things, is an abstraction from concrete particulars, nor are the particulars merely abstractions from a concrete universal...As a result, the temporal order must see a similar relationship between the one and the many as exists in the Eternal One-and-Many." Rousas John Rushdoony, *The Foundations of Social Order: Studies in the Creeds and Councils of the Early Church* (Presbyterian and Reformed Publishing Company, 1968), 13, 91–92.

[116] Luke 3:38.

[117] R. L. Dabney, in countering evolutionary theories regarding the origin of man, aptly described this reality as such: "wherever, in traveling backwards, the domain of creative Omnipotence is met, there true natural science stops." Robert Lewis Dabney, "A Caution against Anti-Christian Science: A Sermon Preached in the Synod of Virginia, October 20, 1871," in *Discussions* 3:134.

regard to that origin. Furthermore, man is a moral being and the kingdom of God is a moral realm, in which citizenship cannot be naturally acquired but only consciously and through good works. Therefore, God has placed Himself in a moral relationship with mankind as its Lawgiver, just as He stands in a natural relationship to mankind as Creator. And there we have the first form of Revelation. It manifests in the natural religious nature of man, through which man lives through God and God lives in man. It is supplemented and completed by Christ's redemptive work, by which he reawakens this previously depraved nature in man and restores the rightful relationship between Himself and mankind—a redemption which serves for man's glory.

God's Revelation of Himself is therefore intrinsically bound to His redemptive work, and both serve the purpose of the establishing the Kingdom of God—the chief and final end of creation. Once this truth is denied the entire organism of nature becomes an inexplicable mystery. And it is precisely for this reason that we reject the sharp distinction made between science and theology, since the purpose of the former is to complement the latter as a key to grow in understanding of the divine plan for creation.

The supernatural is therefore neither foreign nor unrelated to nature. On the contrary, the natural builds upon the supernatural, and supplements and elucidates our understanding thereof.[118] The same laws

---

[118] This sentiment, namely that grace redeems nature, would be echoed later one of Hoedemaker's successors, the great Neo-Calvinist theologian Herman Bavinck, who wrote: "As Redeemer, God follows the same path He does as Creator and Ruler of all things. Grace is something different to nature, but it joins with nature so as not destroy it but rather to renew it. Grace is not an inheritance that is acquired by virtue of natural descent, but it is covenantally maintained through the natural relations embedded in

which characterize the realm of Revelation and by which it is recognized are also applicable to nature, and point to that one plan, that one purpose, that one spirit in all of creation—all of which is directed toward the Man Jesus Christ, the Head of mankind. In this regard both nature and mankind themselves are simply halls in the great palace of God the King.[119]

These same laws and principles which we observe to be at work in nature can also be found at work throughout the history of Revelation. There also we see the unity, the long preparation, the prophetic types, the great harmonious whole to which natural science points.

The central principle of our science and of our theology, might, at first glance, not seem so different from that of naturalism and empiricism. Out of the lower the higher proceeds, modern science and modern theology claim, and we say the same. But when different parties say similar things that does not always necessarily mean or entail the same thing. According to the former two, this is a purely natural, impersonal, and necessary principle. But we regard the principle as standing in direct relation to the divine plan and purpose for creation, which has a distinctly moral dimension. In other words, the whole had already been present at the start and in the seed the ripe fruit was already present. The highest divine purpose was already there at the beginning, as it will be there at the end. The past and the future are both manifestations of the decrees of God. In short: the development and flow of nature is not merely mechanic but organic. And we see this development

---

human nature." Herman Bavinck, *Handleiding bij het onderwijs in den Christelijke godsdienst* (Kok, 1913), 115–16.

[119] The implication here is that God's Kingdom, as the ultimate end for which creation was designed, is much greater than mankind and much greater than nature itself.

even in every plant and in every animal. In the seed the tree is present and in the son the father. Both Scripture and nature reveal this truth, but the naturalists miss this and are therefore unable to not only understand Revelation, but even nature itself.[120]

Let us now proceed to focus on the first, namely Scripture. The entire Bible is a refutation of the naturalist system, since therein we see that from the start the future in its entirety was present and set. Note, for example, the paradise-promise,[121] as therein you will find the whole plan of redemption, and all of history furthermore manifests the covenantal blessings proclaimed to Noah,[122] even in the age of the New Covenant. One can try and deny the supernatural, but it can everywhere be seen. All of history stands in opposition to naturalism, and this is particularly evident in that there is a divine imprint providing

---

[120] Here Hoedemaker makes philosophical arguments pertaining to both *genesiology*, that is, the origin of reality and *teleology*, that is, the purpose of reality.

Genesiology: Naturalists and empiricists regard energy and growth in nature as impersonal, mechanical forces. However, energy always has to have a source, and naturalists and evolutionists cannot and will not account for this source. Only a Christian philosophy of science, in presupposing God, is able to account for the Source of all energy in the universe, Christ, the Logos, in and through Whom all things are provided with the energy necessary to exist and re-produce (Romans 11:36).

Teleology: Because naturalists do not recognize an overarching purpose to reality, since everything evolved at random, they can never have a consistent vision for the direction of civilization nor can they account for the existence of moral principles. Thus, because they can never understand the purpose to nature, namely to reveal and glorify God (Psalm 96:11–12; Romans 1:20), they can never truly understand nature.

[121] Genesis 3:15.

[122] Genesis 9:9–10.

coherence to all of history in which the whole is not simply necessary to provide meaning to the parts, but because in every part the whole can be found. Herein lies the organic as opposed to the mechanical nature thereof.[123]

Botany teaches us that the flower, the root, and the leaf are all merely manifestations of the same basic form. Zoological study can, by simply studying a few remnants of bones, reconstruct how an entire skeleton must have looked. The same can be said regarding the history of Revelation. As long as there remains one word or one act of God, we have a reliable witness from which all others can be derived. If you so desire, take away the tree, but grant us to keep just one branch, even if it has no roots and its leaves will fade. Out of this cutting the tree will grow again.

---

[123] Hoedemaker here describes the basic principle of a distinctly Christian philosophy of history, which had, during his own time, most excellently been embodied by the Dutch Christian historian, Guillaume Groen van Prinsterer (1801–76). Groen van Prinsterer namely held that history itself was pedagogic and, in the long run, reflected the divinely imprinted essence of reality. History provides us with valuable lessons regarding the nature of God-given reality precisely because of its proximate relationship to God's creative-redemptive order and plan for the cosmos: that is, God, as sovereign director of history decrees the flow of history in accordance with both its cosmological *genesis* (or origin) in the divine design of creation as well as its cosmological *telos* (purpose/fulfillment) in the glorification of Christ's Lordship. See Guillaume Groen van Prinsterer, *Ongeloof en Revolutie*, 57, 76–77, 243.

Hoedemaker also distinguishes this Christian philosophy of history in which history is the manifestation of the will and purpose of a living God from secular philosophies of history which attempts to explain the mechanism of and energy behind history by means of natural and impersonal forces, thereby perpetually remaining stuck with secondary causes and consequently being unable to provide any real meaning to history or reality as such.

Some have lamented that many in the church have at times overlooked the distinction between the Old and New Testaments and wrongly gave preference to the former. Well, without becoming an advocate for ignorance, we have to admit that the divine and eternal perspective of the Old Testament is still far superior to the shallow position of our opponents. The truth was there from the beginning—and now that we have seen Him, Jesus, who is the Truth, we find Him in every word of God.

The simple and common Christian speaks and lives Scripture. It is him who is tested by having to bring his own Isaac to the altar, who thereafter he fights with the angel[124] at Jabbok and travels with Israel through the Red Sea, through the desert, to Canaan. That he finds his own life reflected in the Scriptures is to the Christian a more solid evidence of its divine nature than a hundred apologetic works. And even liberal theology, which in its pride mocks such a simple faith, still claims to adhere to what it considers to be the moral lessons of the histories recorded in the Bible. But these lessons are in themselves inseparable from the facts of Divine Revelation in Biblical history itself. In this regard they feed themselves with the very fruit grown on the tree of Revelation.

In the field of religion no one desires to claim originality, since truth itself is so ancient, that even the apostle Paul, in receiving his doctrine by means of divine inspiration, appeals to the example of Abraham in order to confirm the truth of his doctrine regarding justification by faith alone.

---

[124] From the original Dutch it seems evident that Hoedemaker understood this "angel" referenced in Genesis 32:22–32 as a mere angel, although from the text it is evident that it was Christ Himself who had wrestled with Jacob. The very name Israel, which Jacob received following the encounter, means "struggling/wrestling with God."

As soon as our eyes are opened to see the symmetry between the Old and New Testaments,[125] Scripture becomes alive for us and the most glorious Revelation becomes evident to us on every page and in every word. Once you have understood this, you have come to understand the divine organism of Revelation,[126] which is, in all of its parts, as immortal as Milton's angel,[127] so that while it can be "destroyed," it can never be extinguished.[128] As Jan ten Kate[129] has shown us in his lecture on the Psalms, the Old and New Testaments form a harmonious whole, like the different bricks that make up the temple, each of which are placed on their specific place for a specific purpose and each of which supports and carries the other in perfect symmetry. To this we add that, if one of these

---

[125] Hoedemaker therefore rejects any neo-Marcionist or neo-Gnostic notions of a separation between the Revelation contained in the Old and New Testaments and any denial of the divine authority of the former.

[126] When Hoedemaker refers to the "Goddelijk organisme der openbaring," i.e., the divine organism of Revelation, he is referring to the fact that Revelation is alive, effectual, and life-changing, both as an objective reality and subjectively in us through the power of the Holy Spirit who witnesses to its truth in us and by whose power we appropriate that truth.

[127] A reference to John Milton's famous work, *Paradise Lost*.

[128] Here Hoedemaker's distinction between form and content when it comes to Divine Revelation is relevant. The idea conveyed here is that Scripture, in its manifestations as a printed document, or, in our twenty-first-century context as an online document, can be destroyed, but the actual contents thereof can never be destroyed because of the infallible promise of God to verbally preserve his Word (Psalm 12:6–7; Matthew 5:18, 24:35).

[129] Jan Jacob Lodewijk ten Kate (1819–89) was a Dutch Reformed poet and theologian who published in 1864 a widely-read work on the theology of the Psalms and Isaiah, referenced here by Hoedemaker.

bricks were to be discarded at any point in history, then that very stone, in spite of the attacks of the scoffers, would eventually become a cornerstone itself.

Strauss,[130] in recognizing the relationship between the Old and New Testaments which we are now pointing toward, tried to employ it as a means of developing a purely naturalist explanation of the life of Jesus. He argued that the life of Jesus was imagined first by the early Christians and thereafter in the gospels in accordance with examples found in the Old Testament. What an example this is in terms of proving how science, regardless of its aims, eventually confirms Revelation. What a witness the much-feared work of Strauss is for the unity of the Old and New Testaments. Because, yes, in truth, there is in fact a reproduction of the history of the Old Testament in the life of Jesus. But this is a truthful, genuine, and living reproduction and not an artificially created one. The New Testament Revelation was received on the back of the Revelation of the Old Testament. The divine imprint is equally present in both, with the life of Jesus being the fulfillment of the same truths revealed in preceding ages.

Revelation itself is also historical, a historical reality just as much as the history contained in Scripture. It has both a divine and a human character. Its seed and life are eternal, even if its development is historical and temporal. And indeed, it was our opponents who pointed us toward the human character thereof, but in the process we came to an even greater understanding of its truly divine character.[131] For all the questions, which are most

---

[130] David Friedrich Strauss (1808–74), the liberal higher critic.

[131] Hoedemaker is giving too much credit to the scholarly contributions of higher criticism here. It is indeed true that higher critics have emphasized the role of the human authors in the production of Scripture, but this had by no means been denied in

often especially aimed at the Old Testament, such as why the polygamy of the patriarchs was not explicitly condemned by Moses, why imprecatory psalms are considered the genuine Revelation of a loving God, or why there are so little evidence of faith in an afterlife in the Old Testament,[132] we have this one answer: God never disrupts or breaks the unity of this gradual development of Revelation. God takes man, He takes His people, and uses them as He found them in order to, through his sovereign providence and grace, which He both reveals to and works in and through man, creates a new man and a spiritual people, of which we find a type or shadow in the history of Israel.

---

any way in the history of orthodox Christian theology prior to the nineteenth century. As the historical theologian Richard Muller has pointed out, for example: "The Reformers and their scholastic followers all recognized that God must in some way condescend or accommodate Himself to human ways of knowing in order to reveal Himself. This accommodation occurs specifically in the use of human words and concepts for the communication of the law and the gospel, but it in no way implies the loss of truth or the lessening of scriptural authority. The accommodation or condescension refers to the manner or mode of revelation, the gift of the wisdom of the infinite God in finite form, not to the quality of the revelation or to the matter revealed." Richard Muller, *Dictionary of Latin and Greek Theological Terms: Drawn Principally from Protestant Scholastic Theology* (Baker, 2006), 19.

[132] The examples used here by Hoedemaker cannot be regarded as all on the same level when it comes to serving the purpose for which he employs them. While polygamy is shown throughout the Old Testament in terms of its negative and destructive consequences, and implicitly rejected in the New Testament (1 Timothy 3:2, 12; Titus 1:6), the same cannot be said regarding imprecations, a practice which is continued—with divine sanction—under the New Covenant (2 Timothy 4:14). Also, although it is not a major theme in Old Testament texts, the doctrine of the resurrection of the body and the eternal afterlife is expressly taught in texts such as Daniel 12:2.

Revelation does not come to us by means of a series of abstract truths, but through God's establishment of a relationship with sinful man.

The relationship of this Revelation to the purpose for which it has been given by God as it is known by means of his redemptive acts and promises, becomes a light which elucidates itself, nature, life, and the future, and from this clarifying function of Scripture a holistic worldview can be derived.[133] Divine Revelation is, objectively speaking, absolute and perfect, but the perspectives and opinions derived from it are man-made and therefore vary from one time to another and from one nation to the next. Therefore, the subjective reception thereof is gradual and consequently imperfect. Eve did not fully grasp all the Messianic implications of the paradise promise, which was not due to any imperfections in the promise itself, but due to her limited insight. Our Redeemer prophesied His own suffering, death, and resurrection, but the disciples remained reluctant in their understanding and were blinded by prejudice. Truths, revealed to us from outside of ourselves, are not our own. Goethe[134] beautifully expressed this reality as such: "What we have inherited, we must reclaim again in order to own it." And now, precisely because the divine seed of Revelation grows in and through history, we can speak of Revelation as being a historical phenomenon.

---

[133] This principle is known as the *analogia fidei* or *analogia revelationis*, which emphasizes the unity of the Scriptures, nature and reason as integral parts of the Revelation of the same God and in which Scripture provides the framework for the right use of reason and for understanding natural phenomena. Joseph Palakeel, *The Use of Analogy in Theological Discourse: An Investigation in Ecumenical Perspective* (Gregoriana, 1995), 54–55.

[134] German writer and philosopher Johann Wolfgang von Goethe (1749–1832).

What we point to here with regard to Revelation in general also applies to those instances where God personally acts in supernatural ways throughout history. In accordance with the understanding of wonders prevalent among the masses in the ancient world, it would be precisely those unexpected, inexplicable, and fantastic acts which would be most obviously that of the gods. Such an understanding of divine acts does not require order, symbolism, or coherence. But such an understanding cannot be derived from Holy Scripture. Here, the coherence between divine actions and the background to it as the organic prelude to that wonder is always evident. In fact, the deeper we delve into the organism of Revelation, the more evident it becomes that the supernatural is even present in the natural throughout. It cannot always be precisely pointed out, yet it cannot be denied either. In the history of our spiritual lives, in the history of Revelation and in the history of the church the supernatural is always present.

For example, in the supernatural intervention that leads to the conversion of Paul on the way to Damascus must be seen in relation to the hints found in the tale itself and elsewhere in Scripture regarding this persecutor of Christians past. Then it becomes most evident that the supernatural Revelation he then received stands in direct relation to his past.

It is by no means any different with the history of Divine Revelation. And yet, rationalists and naturalists perpetually refuse to forsake the idea of interpreting the history of Revelation as a purely natural phenomenon.[135]

---

[135] In the following few paragraphs, it becomes evident why Hoedemaker places such emphasis on Revelation being a historically mediated reality. Standing in the Christian historicist tradition of the nineteenth century, Hoedemaker's polemics is

Ferdinand Christian Bauer has made it his purpose in his work *The History of Christianity and the Christian Church in the First Three Centuries* to show how wonders and miracles can be explained as purely natural phenomena. Renan did the same with regard to Israel's monotheism, which he explained in terms of their so-called natural tendencies.[136]

But the rationalists had already started expounding such theories even before these men. They have sought to provide a purely natural explanation for a plague such as water of the Nile changing into blood or the journey through the Red Sea. They even went as far as to claim that the Egyptian wizards used stuffed snakeskin for their walking sticks due to the scarcity of wood at the time.

---

aimed, in particular, against the rationalists of the time who maintained that all truths are rational abstractions. Over against this ideal, Hoedemaker maintains history's pedagogic value because of the fact that history is given from outside the human mind as opposed to being the result thereof. In other words, the emphasis here is on the fact that Divine Revelation cannot be regarded as the product of human innovation but is always something that man receives. This argument is foundational to conservatism itself as is evident from the fact that the Irish philosopher Edmund Burke, the father of conservatism, emphasized this same principle by arguing that history itself, as manifestation of divine providence, reflects divine design, sovereignty and purpose. Edmund Burke, *Thoughts on the Prospect of a Regicide Peace: In a Series of Letters* (Owen, 1796), 93.

[136] Ferdinand Christian Bauer (1792–1860) and Ernest Renan (1823–92) were historians of religion and higher critics and also contemporaries of Hoedemaker who denied not only the divine origin of the Bible, but also believed that the Biblical account regarding Jesus's life is a myth. See George Grebens, *Debate Resolved: Evolution, Creation, Intelligent Design and Hybrids* (Xlibris, 2011), 319.

And what was the end result of such attempts? In the first place it has actually confirmed the truth of Holy Scripture beyond any shadow of a doubt, since if it were a purely human invention, its authors would have modified such stories to fit in with their preconceived ideas regarding the supernatural—ideas which are, sadly, shared by many of our contemporaries. Furthermore, it affirms the organic and historical nature of Revelation, since such miracles in Scripture never amount to a distinct break from natural history, but guide and sanctify it, as all of Revelation stands in direct relation to its overarching purpose: God's plan of redemption.

And thus you see the appropriate perspective of the believer toward the new theology and the ethical and scientific objectives of unbelief with regard to the doctrine of Revelation. It is our purpose to utilize those valuable and true findings even of an antagonistic scientific investigation against itself and in service of the faith, and to, in the Name of Jesus Christ, rightly recast it toward His glory. After all, the same materials which were used by the Israelites to create the golden calf were later used to decorate God's tabernacle, and the same source of its gold would later be the source of the gold used for the ark.[137]

Throughout this work I have made it my purpose to trace the main principles and tendencies of Revelation, but allow me to mention one final aspect

---

[137] Here again, Hoedemaker alludes to the reality that there are no uninterpreted facts in the universe. Because natural or general Revelation is available to all men, even unbelievers (Romans 1:18–20), unbelieving scholars and scientists often discover truths by means of their investigation. However, because they do not interpret these facts as they should, i.e., in relation to their Creator, they are most often distorted. It is then the duty of Christian scholars to take such facts and interpret them in light of their relation to God—their proper context without which they cannot be rightly understood.

thereof. Until now, there has been too much of an exclusive emphasis on sacred history as the history of Israel, and too little upon history as the divinely-guided development of the world as a whole. For example, while the preparation for the gospel among our pagan ancestors has often been recognized, the emphasis has almost solely been on the negative character thereof, namely in terms of pointing the nations to their depravity and need of redemption. That was indeed an important aspect of their historical development, but only one aspect thereof. Both the preparation for the gospel among the Israelites and the pagans together form part of one great divine plan for the world.

The table of nations found in Genesis[138] is itself evidence that all of history needs to be understood in terms of God's redemptive purposes. These lineages do not only point to the Jewish people in particular, but to God's providential purposes for all the nations in general. After all, God has not only called Israel to serve Him, but has also, through Israel, called the nations to his service. Israel was preordained to be the vessel of Divine Revelation, but this does not exclude the sanctification of the rest of humanity. Every talent found on earth needs to be cultivated. We find this same truth in the relationship between the nations prior to the flood. Among the descendants of Cain the arts flourished, while Seth and Enoch glorified God in their simplicity—and yet they were preordained to complement each other as seeds complement the field and as the physical complements the spiritual.

In order to achieve this divine purpose, humanity had to be divided into nations. They often strive toward unity, but this cannot and should not be achieved, since it would thwart the very purpose of Revelation. They have been separated into a multitude

---

138 Genesis 10.

of nations, of which each has exhibited its own unique and God-given development. Nations have had to grow and develop on the natural soil that is their natural predispositions and their own abilities as these have been sanctified by Godly principles.[139]

---

[139] This idea, namely that the divinely-ordained social order is national, tribal, or ethnic, rather than imperial and universal, is commonly known as Christian Nationalism or Ethnic Complementarianism. Hoedemaker here explains that national distinctions serve a positive purpose in God's plan of redemption. Christ, with His great commission, also commanded His disciples to evangelize the nations (Matthew 28:19), so that these nations, as covenantal entities, may glorify God, each with their unique abilities, dispositions and talents (Acts 17:26–27). In the eschatological vision of Revelation 7:9–10, nations evidently remain distinct yet redeemed identities making up the glorified Bride of Christ. During the twentieth century the influential Dutch-American theologian and successor of Hoedemaker, Geerhardus Vos, articulated this same idea as such:

> Nationalism, within its proper limits, has the divine sanction; an imperialism that would, in the interest of one people, obliterate all lines of distinction is everywhere condemned as contrary to the divine will. Later prophecy raises its voice against the attempt at world-power, and that not only, as is sometimes assumed, because it threatens Israel, but for the far more principal reason, that the whole idea is pagan and immoral. Now it is through maintaining the national diversities, as these express themselves in the difference of language, and are in turn upheld by this difference, that God prevents realization of the attempted scheme. Besides this, however, a twofold positive divine purpose may be discerned in this occurrence. In the first place there was a positive intent that concerned the natural life of humanity. Under the providence of God each race or nation has a positive purpose to serve, fulfillment of which depends on relative seclusion from others. And secondly, the events at this

There exists also a negative aspect of the historical development of Revelation, as opposed to its positive development with the nation of Israel. According to Joshua 14:2 it was precisely because the light of earlier Revelation had vanquished among other nations that Israel was uniquely called to be sanctified as the people of God. For this same reason Abraham had been called away from his home and his people in Ur of the Chaldeans. Later his son Isaac was born, not as the result of the natural course of life but as a gift of grace. And this same principle was at work in circumcision as sign of the covenant, membership of which was acquired on the basis not of natural descent but of the sovereign predestination of God. It can also be seen in the sacrifice of Isaac, which was replaced by the sacrifice of an animal, through which both father and son had been devoted to God. The spiritual and the natural were constantly at work and cooperated in the sanctification of Israel's national life. This can be seen in Egypt where not only Moses but all of Israel developed the cultural soil on which the seed of Revelation could find fertile ground. Later the same process was at work in the Assyrian and Babylonian captivities.

Yet all the world's nations have been schooled by their own historical experience, with each contributing in their own way. The Romans played a major role in developing a legal system that proved beneficial for the education of the more rugged nations. The Greeks contributed immensely to the

---

stage were closely interwoven with the carrying out of the plan of redemption. They led to the election and separate living of one race and one people. Election from its very nature presupposes the existence of a larger number from among which the choice can be made. (Geerhardus Vos, *Biblical Theology: Old and New Testaments* [Eerdmans, 1948], 72).

arts, sciences, and literature. The contribution of the peoples of Asia in terms of the development of philosophy is undeniable.

The positive results of all of these contributions are then united with those of Israel in the New Testament Christian Church, and later in the migrations of European tribes, the Crusades, and also in the Reformation. But the development of humanity as a whole and each of its national constitutive parts is not yet complete, and it will one day encompass all of creation. Until then, all expressions of our faith are to be counted only as preliminary as are all attempts at an infallible science, which merely anticipates the future.

Within the Roman Church, however, we find a good example of the manifestation of the age-old Babelist ambition of indiscriminate unity without diversity. The fullness of the time has indeed come, but the fulness of the nations is to be anticipated in the future. Like the pagan nations of old, today Christian nations and Christian races are in the process of cultivating their own unique aptitudes and abilities, each in their unique way, under the guidance of the Holy Spirit. England and America, Germany and the Norse peoples, Italy, France, yes even the smaller nations like the Netherlands and Switzerland, each have their own unique destiny and calling. The east had contributed to the development of ancient Israel, but is yet to bring their contributions to the foot of the cross.

If we are not being mistaken, we are now witnessing the final turning point in the history of Revelation. All these contributions will eventually come together. Witness how the believers are currently exiled among all nations. In the future, these believers will be added together through the only force that can bring them to unity and transform them into the Kingdom of God. This is how world unity will be achieved, but this unity is not the unity of Babel but the unity of Jerusalem. It is a unity of faith in and knowledge of Christ, the perfect Son of man, because then the fullness of the nations will become the fullness of Christ. Only through Him this earth will be renewed and glorified and transformed into the habitation of the new, redeemed mankind. Just as Christ's human body has been prophetically glorified, so this world will one day arise from its present predicament and humiliation.[140] Then the words of the hymn will ring true regarding this world:

> Her sins wiped out, her captives free;
> Her voice a music unto thee.[141]

For now, we have seen only the shadow of the fullness of Revelation. But in this hymn we sing about the fulfillment of the history of Revelation. And even this hymn of redeemed humanity is merely one of the voices that will make up the glorious accords of eternity.

---

[140] Hoedemaker here concludes this work with a distinctly optimistic eschatology, which is often termed Postmillennialism, that is, the belief that Christ will only return after a future period of glory for Christendom as it prospers all over the globe and all the nations of the world have come to repentance and faith in Christ as King.

[141] The distinctly postmillennial nature and implications of these lyrics quoted here by Hoedemaker are particularly evident when viewed in light of the entirety of this traditional nineteenth-century hymn's verse:

> I ask no heaven till earth be Thine;
> Nor glory crown while work of mine,
> Remaineth here. When earth shall shine
> Among the stars, her stains wiped out, her captives free,
> Her songs sweet music unto Thee—
> For crown give, Lord, new work to me.

Epilogue

*The Continuing Relevance of
Hoedemaker's Philosophy of Revelation*

Admittedly, some aspects of the way in which Hoedemaker frames his philosophy of Revelation might come across as strange to the twenty-first-century reader. However, this in itself should be cause for pause in order to ask ourselves if we have not become too much accustomed to the prevailing (and failing) modern and postmodern worldviews that have shaped society throughout all of our lifetimes. Our appreciation of the role of divine sovereignty and the authority of Scripture in Hoedemaker's philosophy of history should really go without saying, but the same can perhaps not be said regarding, for example, his distinct emphasis on the historical nature of Revelation itself.

At the heart of this historicist emphasis in Hoedemaker's epistemology lies his conviction that history, as the providential manifestation of divinely created ordinances, manifest the will of God. This is a distinctly traditionalist or conservative point of view, by which long-term durability and workability serve as confirmations of the fact that something is in accordance with divine purposes, and therefore history itself is understood as a means by which God reveals Himself.

Of course, within a non-Christian Romanticist framework, such a traditionalist view would of course be a ludicrous position to take. It could, for example, in order to remain consistent, entail arguing that the practice of abortion on demand would be in accordance with natural laws, since it has been successfully implemented for decades and therefore constitutes a historically acquired right. This was also one of the primary reasons why Dooyeweerd, for example, later distanced himself from the Christian historicism of Groen van Prinsterer and Hoedemaker.

However, it must be admitted that understanding history's revelatory and pedagogic function within the framework of an infallible Revelation, that is, Scripture, makes for a distinctly Christian traditionalist conservative position which, I would argue, represents a holistic worldview that fully accords with Christian orthodoxy. When Scripture provides the framework, history can be understood in terms of the covenantal and eschatological purposes of God as revealed in Scripture. In other words, Scripture provides the framework for understanding history just like it provides the framework for understanding every other aspect of reality.

Moreover, there is an important epistemic implication of Hoedemaker's philosophy of Revelation, namely, that truth itself is not merely an abstraction that is self-evident to the human mind. Truth, being ever dependent upon Revelation, is never something that the individual acquires by means of rational contemplation or empirical observation, but is always a reality that is provided to us by means of the Holy Spirit convincing us of certain propositions. It is precisely to emphasize this God-given nature of truth that Hoedemaker, in his historical context, emphasizes the pedagogic value of history.

However, it is only if the premise of the infallibility of Scripture as Divine Revelation is accepted, that history does in fact make sense and have pedagogic value. The failure of all anti-Christian endeavors of the past can then, within a Biblical framework, be rightly understood as a testimony to the fact that disobedience to God inevitably leads to self-destruction (Deuteronomy 28:15–68). Furthermore, this Presuppositionalist Traditionalism also serves as a logical theological and narrative precedent for an optimistic of postmillennialist eschatology, something for which Hoedemaker, in his historical context, stands out from among his fellow Dutch Anti-Revolutionary and Neo-Calvinist contemporaries. Whereas Bavinck, for example, calls the idea of "gradual progress in world history" a "chiliast dream"[142] and holds to a pessimistic vision of the future in which there will be large-scale apostasy preceding the return of Christ,[143] one finds a distinct optimism in Hoedemaker's long-term vision for the future, in which the gospel will sanctify all the nations of the earth.[144]

This eschatological difference wasn't immaterial for Hoedemaker's dispute with Bavinck and Kuyper over Article 36 of the Belgic Confession. After all, the original wording of the confession, supported by Hoedemaker, expressly states the that the purpose of the government's duty to "remove and prevent all idolatry and false worship," is so "that the kingdom of the antichrist may be thus destroyed." This has distinct eschatological implications which did not sit well with Bavinck and Kuyper, but which Hoedemaker understood to be necessary in order to truly fulfill the

---

[142] Bavinck, *Christelijke wetenschap*, 57: "een gestadigen vooruitgang," "chiliastische droom."

[143] Herman Bavinck, *Gereformeerde Dogmatiek: vierde deel* (J. H. Bos), 460.

[144] Philippus Jacobus Hoedemaker, *Het evangelie van het Oude Verbond: Opstellen over de Openbaring Gods onder het Oude Verbond* (Sneek, 1889), 33.

Christian calling to exercise dominion over every sphere of life.

While Kuyper's vision of culture has rightly been garnering a lot of interest in the English-speaking world over the past several decades, Hoedemaker's contribution still remains too much neglected. The Kuyperian idea of common grace as equally maintaining the conditions for knowledge and the use of the empirical and rational faculties for both the regenerate as well as the unregenerate, led him to embrace a pluralistic or multicultural vision for society in which Christianity is but a guiding and sanctifying ingredient.[145] Bavinck likewise maintained that the state has no authority in establishing the Christian religion as he regarded religious convictions as epistemically distinct from objective knowledge.[146]

Hoedemaker, in disagreeing with Kuyper and Bavinck's premise, counters that since there exists no unrevealed knowledge in all of the universe, it is only Christianity that can bring about true socio-cultural progress, while all other worldviews only maintain themselves inasmuch as they borrow capital from Christianity. For this reason, the public exercise of any non-Christian religions in society is not only at odds with the commandments of God, but detrimental to genuine societal progress itself. In this regard Hoedemaker's doctrine of theonomy, that is, his conviction that Biblical Law provides the absolute moral standard for all spheres of society in all times and contexts, was more consistently anti-liberal than that of Bavinck or Kuyper.

Finally, Hoedemaker's emphasis on the historicity of Revelation also speaks to the undeniable reality that the Bible itself is a historically shaped and historically

---

[145] Abraham Kuyper, *De gemeene gratie in Wetenschap en Kunst* (Höveker, 1905), 27.
[146] Bavinck, *Christelijke Wetenschap*, 94.

preserved document. The Bible is an infallible record of God's Revelation of Himself through history. The fact that the Bible not only came to be within the context of history, but also that its infallible text has also been historically preserved over millennia, is a testimony to how God as Creator of time and space, sovereignly and, without ever being impeded, directs all of history for His purposes. This emphasis needs to be understood in terms of Hoedemaker's polemical objectives in the nineteenth century—in particular the higher critical reduction of the Bible to a purely human document—but it remains ever-relevant to all Christians in every time and place who hold to the Bible as the infallible Word of God which authoritatively provide our lives of direction and purpose and reveal the path of Salvation in Christ.

Nonetheless, while there is great value in Hoedemaker's Christian historicism, especially given the context in which he wrote, one distinct weakness of his epistemology is his failure to fully realize the propositional nature thereof. Propositions can, after all, only be understood through the use of logic, a fundamental building block of all human thought. That being said, however, I don't believe that Hoedemaker's epistemology, especially given his appreciation of history as the manifestation of divine decrees, is necessarily at odds with how the Reformed philosopher Gordon Clark (1902—85) describes the propositional nature of Revelation when he states that

> in all other varieties of truth, God must be accounted sovereign. It is his decree that makes one proposition true and another false. Whether the proposition be physical, psychological, moral or theological, it is God

> who made it that way. A proposition is true because God thinks it so.[147]

Hoedemaker rightly emphasizes that because God is sovereign over history, all of history—from the very foundation of the world unto its final culmination—serves his primary purpose with all of creation, the glorification of Jesus Christ. Despite all assaults upon the faith, Christ's Kingdom will perpetually remain not only invincible, but continue to expand over the world and sanctify it, since God's plan of redemption of all creation in Christ (Isaiah 11:1–9; Romans 11:36) is confirmed by his infallible promises and the absolute sovereignty with which he directs all of history. And since, as believers, we are the followers, disciples and soldiers of Jesus Christ, we can take heart even in the midst of the most tumultuous times and circumstances, that God is not only in control of every aspect of the past, the present and the future, but is also always working and directing all things together for our good (Romans 8:28), since we are part of the victorious Kingdom of Christ.

---

[147] Gordon Clark, *Logic* (The Trinity Foundation, 1985), 106.

Index

Scripture Index

Bibliography

Aalders, Willem. *Revolutie en Réveil 1789–1989*. J. N. Voorhove, 1989.

Alvarado, Ruben. "Introduction." In P. J. Hoedemaker, *Reformed Ecclesiology in an Age of Denominationalism*, translated by Ruben Alvarado. Pantokrator Press, 2019.

Alvarado, Ruben. "Preface." In P. J. Hoedemaker, *Article 36 of the Belgic Confession Vindicated against Dr. Abraham Kuyper: A Critique of his Series on Church and State in "Common Grace"*, translated by Ruben Alvarado. Pantokrator Press, 2019.

Bavinck, Herman. "Review van 'Niet van eigen uitlegging' door Ph.J. Hoedemaker." *De Bazuin* 34, no. 51 (1886).

Bavinck, Herman. *Christelijke Wetenschap*. Kok, 1904.

Bavinck, Herman. *Wijsbegeerte der Openbaring*. Kok, 1908.

Bavinck, Herman. *Handleiding bij het onderwijs in den Christelijke godsdienst*. Kok, 1913.

Bremmer, Rolf. "Historische aspecten van de Afscheiding." In *Aspecten van de Afscheiding*, edited by A. de Groot and P. Schram. Wever, 1984.

Bullinger, Heinrich. *Anklag und erstliches ermanen Gottes Allmachtigen zu eyner gemeynnen Eydgenosschaft*. Froschauer, 1544.

Burke, Edmund. *Thoughts on the Prospect of a Regicide Peace: In a Series of Letters.* Owen, 1796.

Carr, David. *Experience and History: Phenomenological Perspectives on the Historical World.* Oxford University Press, 2014.

Clark, Gordon. *A Christian Philosophy of Education.* Eerdmans, 1946.

Clark, Gordon. *Logic.* The Trinity Foundation, 1985.

Dabney, Robert Lewis. *Discussions, Volume III: Philosophical.* Ross House, 1980.

Dabney, Robert Lewis. *On Secular Education.* Canon Press, 1996.

Dooyeweerd, Herman. *De wijsbegeerte der wetsidee. Boek I: De wetsidee als grondlegging der wijsbegeerte.* H. J. Paris, 1935.

Dooyeweerd, Herman. *Vernieuwing en Bezinning om het Reformatorische Grondmotief.* J. B. Van den Brink & Co, 1959.

Grebens, George. *Debate Resolved: Evolution, Creation, Intelligent Design and Hybrids.* Xlibris, 2011.

Groen van Prinsterer, Guillaume. *Beschouwingen over staats- en volkenrecht, I: Proeve over de middelen waardoor de waarheid wordt gekend en gestaafd.* S & J Luchtmans, 1834.

Groen van Prinsterer, Guillaume. *Handboek der Geschiedenis van het Vaderland, volume I.* Höveker, 1852.

Groen van Prinsterer, Guillaume. *Ongeloof en Revolutie (1847).* Edited by Roel Kuiper and Arie Kuiper. Nederlands Dagblad, 2008.

Groen van Prinsterer, Guillaume. *Nederlandsche Gedachten, 2nd series—V.* Höveker, 1873.

Harinck, Greorge. *Mijn reis was geboden: Abraham Kuypers Amerikaanse tournee.* Verloren, 2009.

Hoedemaker, Philippus Jacobus. *Het probleem der Vrijheid en het theïstisch godsbegrip.* Höveker, 1867.

Hoedemaker, Philippus Jacobus. *Het feit en de geschiedenis der openbaring: eene voorlezing.* Höveker, 1871.

Hoedemaker, Philippus Jacobus. *Handboek voor het onderwijs in het Oude Testament ten dienste van het catechisatie, het huisgezin en de zondagschool.* Höveker, 1886.

Hoedemaker, Philippus Jacobus. *Eenvoudige onderwijzing in de christelijke leer naar de belijdenis der Hervormde Kerk.* Sneek, 1892.

Hoedemaker, Philippus Jacobus. *De Mozaïsche oorsprong der wetten in de boeken Exodus, Leviticus en Numeri: lezingen over de moderne Schriftkritiek des Ouden Testaments.* Daamen, 1895.

Hoedemaker, Philippus Jacobus. *Heel de kerk en heel de volk! Een protest tegen het optreden der Gereformeerden als partij, en een Woord van afscheid aan de Confessionele Vereeniging.* Sneek, 1897.

Hoedemaker, Philippus Jacobus. *Nationaal niet clericaal.* Sneek, 1897.

Hoedemaker, Philippus Jacobus. *Christus voor de rechtbank: der moderne wetenschap.* Daamen, 1898.

Janse, Maartje. "Vereeniging en verlangen om vereenigd te werken—Réveil en civil society." In *Opwekking van de natie: Het protestantse Réveil in Nederland*, edited by Fred van Licburg. Verloren, 2012.

Kant, Immanuel. *Die Religion innerhalb der Grenzen der blossen Vernunft.* Nicolovius, 1793.

Kirpestein, Jan-Willem. *Groen van Prinsterer als belijder van Kerk en Staat in de negentiende eeuw.* Groen & Zoon, 1993.

Kloes, Andrew. *The German Awakening: Protestant Renewal After the Enlightenment, 1815–1848.* Oxford University Press.

Kluit, Elizabeth. *Het Réveil in Nederland: 1817–1854.* H. J. Paris, 1937.

Kuyper, Abraham. *Ons Program.* J. A. Wormser, 1892.

Kuyper, Abraham. *Encyclopaedie der heilige godgeleerdheid, tweede deel: Algemeen deel.* Kok, 1909.

Locke, John. *The Second Treatise of Civil Government.* Edited by Andrew Baily. Broadview Press, 2015.

McCoy, Charles, and Wayne Baker. *Fountainhead of Federalism: Heinrich Bullinger and the Covenantal Tradition.* Westminster/John Knox, 1991.

Muller, Richard. *Dictionary of Latin and Greek Theological Terms: Drawn Principally from Protestant Scholastic Theology.* Baker, 2006.

Palakeel, Joseph. *The Use of Analogy in Theological Discourse: An Investigation in Ecumenical Perspective.* Gregoriana, 1995.

Paul, Mart-Jan. "Hoedemaker en de uitleg van de bijbel." In *Hoedemaker herdacht,* edited by G. Abma and J. de Bruijn. Ten Have, 1989.

Rushdoony, Rousas John. *The Foundations of Social Order: Studies in the Creeds and Councils of the Early Church.* Presbyterian and Reformed Publishing Company, 1968.

Van Dam, Cornelius. *God and Government: Biblical Principles for Today—An Introduction and Resource.* Wipf & Stock, 2011.

Van Dyke, Harry. *Groen van Prinsterer's Lectures in Unbelief and Revolution.* Wedge, 1989.

Van Til, Cornelius. *The Defense of the Faith.* Presbyterian and Reformed Publishing, 1967.

Van Til, Cornelius. *Introduction to Systematic Theology.* Second edition. Presbyterian and Reformed Publishing, 1974.

Van Til, Cornelius. "Letter to Francis Schaeffer, 11 March 1969." *Ordained Servant* 6, no. 4 (1997): 77–80.

Van Vliet, W. G. F. *Groen van Prinsterers Historische benadering van de politiek.* Verloren, 2008.

Van Wyk, Daan. "PJ Hoedemaker: Wat ek bedoel, is die behoud van die kerk." *HTS* 46, no. 4 (1990): 497–512.

Van Wyk, Daan. "P J Hoedemaker, teoloog en kerkman." *HTS* 47, no. 4 (1991): 1069–87.

Vos, Geerhardus. *Biblical Theology: Old and New Testaments.* Eerdmans, 1948.

Vree, Jasper. "Het Réveil als partij in de Nederlandse samenleving: opkomst, groei, doorwerking en geschiedschrijving (1833–1891)." In *Opwekking van de natie: Het protestantse Réveil in Nederland*, edited by Fred van Lieburg. Verloren, 2012.

Woldring, H. E. S. *Een handvol filosofen: Geschiedenis van de filosofiebeoefening aan de Vrije Universiteit in Amsterdam van 1880 tot 2012.* Verloren, 2013.

ABOUT THE REFCON PRESS

RefCon Press is the publishing arm of The Reformed
Conservative where our goal is to share and defend the
conservative heritage of the Reformed faith and follow in
the footsteps of Edmund Burke, Abraham Kuyper, and
Francis Schaeffer—we yearn for a Biblical response to a
world without hope.

The Reformed Conservative is a nonprofit organization and
relies on your tax-deductible gifts. Learn more about us and
donate, at www.thereformedconsertive.org.